THE IMPOSSIBLE DREAM

Miracle Road to Success

THE
IMPOSSIBLE
DREAM

Miracle Road to Success

Jasper Fullard Jr.

ARPress
ILLUMINATING IDEAS.
EMPOWERING VOICES

ARPress
45 Dan Road Suite 5
Canton MA 02021

Hotline: 1(888) 821-0229
Fax: 1(508) 545-7580

Ordering Information:
Quantity sales. Special discounts are available on quantity purchases by corporations, associations, and others. For details, contact the publisher at the address above.

Printed in the United States of America.
ISBN-13:   Paperback   979-8-89356-561-4
              eBook   979-8-89356-563-8
              Hardback   979-8-89356-562-1

Library of Congress Control Number: 2024902493

Contents

DEDICATION

To my family—
my wife, children, and grand children

 # INTRODUCTION

This book will illustrate how a poor Black boy promised his mother that he would one day become a doctor after watching his mother almost die from a nosebleed because of lack care by a White doctor. At the time, I was about eleven years old. Growing up in a family of eleven children, this was considered an impossibility, especially considering that there was little or no inspiration that I could receive from my immediate environment. There were no Black doctors, nurses, or other Black professionals to give me hope of being anything other than a janitor, farmer, or caring for the White man's yard.

I hope the readers of this will receive inspiration and will recognize the role that faith in God played, and the miracle that occurred in overcoming the struggle, and the many obstacles that I faced. By reading this, you will gain strength, courage, and be inspired to overcome your challenges and struggles in life. The promise to my mother was what drove and pushed me along this long and crooked journey. With the thought of so many Black people not being able to receive adequate health care because of racial discrimination was not acceptable. As you read about this story, you may be able to identify with my experience as a poor boy with very low self-esteem. I was from a very poor environment, low educational background, and from a large family but had a strong desire and determination to succeed in life. I never forgot what drove me to pursue a medical degree and the promise that I made to my mother, which is why I dedicated a lot of my time to volunteering in the Black community doing workshop, seminars, and health discussion in the Black churches.

Chapter 1

Zebina, Georgia

I was only four years old when our family left Zebina, so information in this part of the book about Zebina was obtained by collaboration with older family members.

Zebina was a very small country town with less than five hundred people and best defined by farmland, horses, and wagons that traveled along narrow dirt roads, transporting cotton to the gin located a few miles away. There were only two general stores in Zebina that sold clothes, food, hardware, and some farm equipment. You could probably find almost anything in these two stores. In Zebina, if you walk around all day, you may never see a motor vehicle, and there were one or two gas station or gas pumps. Blacks knew their place and where they could or not go, and it seemed as if we all had the same name, "colored boy."

My father had to endure lots of humiliation in order to earn a living for us. He worked as a farmer with very little reward, and the family worked hard harvesting the crops, but we had very little to show for our hard work. Our family was large, and the older member's responsibility was to work hard to help provide for the family. Farming was our means of survival. We would wake up at five to six o'clock in the morning, preparing to go to the field to chop or pick cotton, and usually, there was no breakfast before going to the fields; lunch consisted of bread, bologna, cheese and water. There was never enough food, and we had to work until sundown.

Being a part of a large family had its disadvantages; when time to eat, many times, there was not enough food to go around. We had to work hungry most of the time, and some of us appeared to be under weight or malnourished. The family worked hard, but our parents still struggled to keep food on the table and clothes for us to wear.

I do not believe that we would have survived without farm work. Our mother also later worked as a maid and would bring home leftover food and used clothes for us. Later, my father obtained a job in Augusta, Georgia, at Fort Gordon Army Base. It is still a mystery as to how he got back and forth to work, and I am not sure how long this job lasted before he went back to farming.

There were five boys and two girls at that time were in need of shelter, food, clothes, and school supplies. The school in Zebina was a four-room dilapidated building, approximately three miles from our house. The road was a narrow dirt road, and when it rained, the road was muddy with large water holes, which created significant obstacles getting to and from school.

In Zebina, living conditions were very poor for a family of seven children a mother and father. We lived in a small four room house with holes in the roof and walls, with an outside toilet several yards from the house. The boys had a room, the girls had a room, our parents had their room, and we had a small kitchen. The roof leaked, and you could see outside through the roof and the walls. Winters were very cold, but several people sleeping in one bed had its advantages in keeping each other warm. However, sometimes, you may wake up wet from one of the boys wetting the bed, and usually no one accepted the responsibility for it.

My father had his own way of dealing with a very depressing situation by getting drunk every weekend and coming home late at night, angry, cursing everyone especially my mother. He would also call her degrading names, beat her many times causing bleeding and swelling of her face. We had to watch this happen to her almost every weekend. It was hard watching her go through this over and over again. My father would sometimes find reasons to beat us for something we did or did not do. As a young boy, I did not understand why he would get drunk, abuse us and our mother, and usually spend all of his money on alcohol and other things, rather than things we so desperately needed. Many years later, I began to understand why he did this; with seven children at that time to provide for, my father did the best he could, but it was not enough. And it was his way of reacting to our poor economic situation.

He could not confront his boss about the way he was cheating and mistreating him as a sharecropper. Watching him go through this did not make him a good role model for us. But later, he met a roofer who hired him to help replace roofs on houses in Florida, which required that he would leave us behind in order to make a better living for us. We also saw this as a relief from the stress and agony of his drinking problem. The pay was so much better than farming, and he was able to send money home for my mother to save for what he thought was to buy a car, but Mother had a different plan. Recognizing the need to improve our living conditions, she saved the money to buy a house without my father's knowledge. If he had known, it would have caused a big fight with verbal and physical abuse to my mother. In spite of all the bad things that he did to my mother, she never talked bad about him, and she would not allow us to talk bad about him. She would say, "Your daddy is a good man."

While my father was in Florida, my mother and my older brothers went to Wrens, Georgia, to look at houses. Wrens was about five or six miles from Zebina with a population of twelve hundred. My mother made a down payment on a house using the money she had received from my father that he thought was to go toward purchasing a car. When he came home from Florida and found out that Mother had used all the money for a down payment on a house in Wrens, he was very upset and as usual, wanted to physically abuse her. After seeing the house, he was please and later would boast to his friends about how he was taking care of his family by buying a house in Wrens, Georgia.

We were so surprised and happy about moving to the "big town" of Wrens. To us, we thought it meant no more holes in the ceiling and walls, no more rats and roaches, but we soon learned that we would still have an outside toilet, just like in Zebina. My older brother who had gone with Mother to look at the house was trying to explain to the rest of us how we would get our water at our new house.

He stated, "All you have to do is turn a knob, and water would come out." This was new and exciting to us to know that we would not have to draw water from a well to bathe and cook with.

Moving to Wrens did not change our economic situation very much, but it was certainly a move in the right direction. We had dreams of having our own bed and not having to sleep with four or five of us on a bed. I'm sure my brothers were looking forward to this because I was a bed wetter, which created a big problem. When there were several people sleeping on the same bed, it was very hard to determine who had wet the bed. We all sometimes got a whipping for bed-wetting because of me, and I'm sure my brothers received several whippings that I should have gotten because I would never tell the truth until my mother decided to whip us all. After I was older, I would get up early and change the sheets, which did save a few of whippings until my mother figured this out, knowing that I would not usually make up the bed that early before she got up. And from that point on, I would usually get a whipping every morning before going to school for wetting the bed.

Although we were very poor, I was told of one interesting story in the Fullard family. My grandfather, Americus Fullard, was short in stature but a big man in town because he owned 135 acres of land and was a fairly successful farmer in a town called Sugar Hill, just a few miles from Wrens. He was probably the first Black man in town to own a car. This made my father and my uncles very popular with others in the area. He also owned a store that sold a little of everything, and my older brother would talk about how he would go to help him in the store, and how he would eat lots of candy, and drink sodas all days.

Several years ago, I was told by a White man from the area that he owned the 135 acres of land previously owned by my grandfather. According to him, my grandfather had borrowed $800 from a businessman, who at that time was considered a friend. The 135 acres of land was used a collateral, and my grandfather was unable to repay the loan and lost all 135 acres. After many years, the Fullard sign still hangs over the little store building. Whenever I would go home, this White man would appear trying to get us interested in taking back the land.

We have very little historical information about other relatives on my grandfather's side. He died before we could find out the full history of the land and the full history of Fullard family. It is unfortunate that we do not have pictures to show our children. I have been asked by my children to see pictures of my father and have to tell them that I do not have any pictures of my father or any of his relatives.

Chapter 2

Our New Home

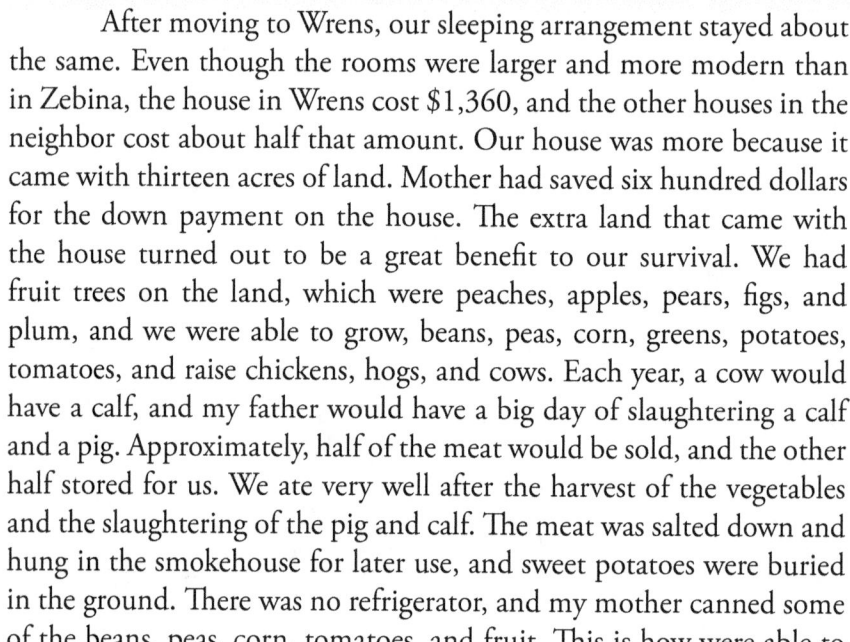

After moving to Wrens, our sleeping arrangement stayed about the same. Even though the rooms were larger and more modern than in Zebina, the house in Wrens cost $1,360, and the other houses in the neighbor cost about half that amount. Our house was more because it came with thirteen acres of land. Mother had saved six hundred dollars for the down payment on the house. The extra land that came with the house turned out to be a great benefit to our survival. We had fruit trees on the land, which were peaches, apples, pears, figs, and plum, and we were able to grow, beans, peas, corn, greens, potatoes, tomatoes, and raise chickens, hogs, and cows. Each year, a cow would have a calf, and my father would have a big day of slaughtering a calf and a pig. Approximately, half of the meat would be sold, and the other half stored for us. We ate very well after the harvest of the vegetables and the slaughtering of the pig and calf. The meat was salted down and hung in the smokehouse for later use, and sweet potatoes were buried in the ground. There was no refrigerator, and my mother canned some of the beans, peas, corn, tomatoes, and fruit. This is how were able to survive.

I remember very well when we first moved to our house in Wrens, Georgia; we were just like kids in a candy store, running around the house, checking everything out. For the first time, we had our own yard to play in and other children to play with. We played baseball, kickball, marbles, and other games. My brothers and I discovered the water faucet; we would turn the water on and run around playing in the water that was running down the road. We were having so much fun until our father saw what we were doing, and the fun stopped when he informed us that he had to pay for the water. We all received a whipping; this was our initiation to our new home.

Our house became the "big house" on the hill where everyone gathered every day. Our neighbors were very friendly, and we became a very close community. We all looked out for each other, and my mother became well-known in the community. She would cook and share food with the neighbors, even though we sometimes didn't have enough for ourselves. Everyone thought my mother was a very caring person because of this but we thought she was mean, especially when she would demand that we stop playing, and be in the house before the sun went down, even though we would be playing in front of our house. We thought we could "out smart" her by sneaking on the porch and sitting down and declaring we had been sitting there before the sun went down. She insisted that we had to be in the house before the sun went down and not just on the porch. I cannot tell you how many whipping my brothers and I received because of this stipulation.

Although we were in a new town with a new house, our economic condition was still the same. We still had to work hard to survive. The word must have gotten around that the new Fullard family could pick a bail of cotton a day, the "cotton picking truck" started stopping by our home everyday looking for people to pick cotton. This was our main means of survival, and we had to pick cotton until after thanksgiving each year. We did not start school until after Thanksgiving, after all the cotton had been picked. Sometimes, the "boss" would allow my father to have the cotton that was left in the fields after Thanksgiving, and we would have to go back to gather what little cotton was left, which usually was not enough to justify taking us back out of school. We would have already missed September, October, and November. This created a tremendous problem for us in school, and we had to study hard to catch up with the other students.

Mother had three more boys and one girl after moving to the new house. I remember when we would see a little old lady with a black bag come to the house. Mother would tell all of us to go up the street and play with our friends. This was quite unusual for her to tell us to go play away from the house, and when we return home, we would hear a baby crying. We thought that the little old lady brought the baby to my mother in the little black bag. We told mother that we did not want the little lady to come back again with that little black bag because every time she comes, she would bring a baby, and we didn't want any more babies. We were much older when we learned what had really happened.

After the birth of my three brothers and one sister, the number of children increased to ten, and we all had to occupy the same two rooms. More space was desperately needed to accommodate everyone. Plans for renovation were initiated by my mother. Shortly after we moved to Wrens, my mother obtained a job at Fort Gordon Army Base in Augusta, Georgia. She started saving money from her job at Fort Gordon, and my oldest brother, who was in the army, sent money. We worked hard picking cotton, and my father was able to obtain a job in construction work. However, this did not last very long, he was fired for cursing out his boss. Mother was able to save enough money to add two additional rooms, and the little side porch was converted to an inside bathroom. We were all very happy about our accomplishments, and one of my brothers was so excited about the bathroom that he would tell neighbors that we didn't have to go outside to "pee" anymore. All we have to do is lift the lid and "pee" in the stool.

Chapter 3

Wrens Elementary and High School

Wrens Elementary and High School was an old, dilapidated, wooden building with approximately five large rooms that could be divided into smaller rooms by pulling a divider across the floor. There was a large wood and coal heater in the middle of the floor, and classes were usually interrupted so that one of us could go out and get wood or coal. We would have classes around the heater. The books were old and outdated, they were "hand me downs" from the White schools located less than two miles away. We also received old, half spoiled cheese and fruit from the White school.

When I would pass by this school, I wondered why we did not have some of the things that they had. Why did we not have new up to date books and food like the White school. However, we were expected to take the same state and national examination as the White students and be graded the same but with less study materials. The classes had too many students, and the conditions less that desirable. The teachers did an outstanding job with what they had to work with. The principal was very strict, and if you were sent to his office, you knew you were going to receive the paddle. And you did not tell you mother because our mother would give us another whipping. I can still see that "mean" look on the principal's face, he never smiled and never complemented you on anything. We were afraid of him. He was well known for his strict discipline. Knowing the condition at Wrens High School, one could understand how some of the students wanted to give up and drop out of school. But if you were able to endure these conditions, after graduation, you could compete with other students from larger schools, and more modern White schools. I give all the credit to our mother and the teachers who were so dedicated to the students at Wrens High School.

Four teachers pose beside the old building. Left to right, Cora Cooper Kelley, Edith Stephens, Amy Hannah, Walton Brown.

The only thing that helped me get through these situations was the dedicated teachers we had in our school. Our teachers were determined not to allow the condition of our building, outdated books, and the fact that most of my classmates and I may not have had breakfast, or lunch most days, keep us from getting a good education. My teachers believed that they could overcome these situations by taking personal interest in our lives. They would spend lunch hours and after school hours tutoring me and the others. I had a very serious speech impediment, and I had trouble pronouncing words starting with "t h" and "s t r" After spending many after school and lunch hours, I still have not overcome this problem, but it was because of their dedication, drive, personal commitment, and concern that made me want to do more and to be "somebody" one day. There were times when I thought the teachers had gone too far when they would go to my home, usually getting there before me, and would be talking to my mother. This was good when I had done well in the class, but , there were times when I knew I was in trouble, and I would go directly to my room and put on an extra pair of pants, preparing for the whipping, that I knew was coming. It did not take long for my mother to figure this out, and she would make me pull down both pair of pants and bypass the installation. For that, I would hate the teacher until I realized that she was interested in me and wanted me to learn to be the best that I could be. I soon realized that putting on two pairs of pants was not the right decision.

Wrens Elementary and High School had many good and some sad memories. When I was in the fifth grade, I developed a very close friendship with one of my classmates. He and I devised a way to use large gallon cans to make music. We would play songs for other students, and we would meet under the highway overpass every morning to practice our skills, usually around eight o'clock in the morning before school. One morning, I arrived at our usual site to practice, but my friend never showed up. As I was making my way to the school, I saw students gathering outside, and an ambulance was backed up to the school. I was told that my closest friend had been shot and killed. I learned later that one of the teachers had a loaded gun in his desk drawer, and my friend removed the gun and was looking at it. About this time, a man delivering soda to the school took the gun from my friend. The gun fired killing my closest friend.

That was very hard for me to overcome for a long time; I had very low self-esteem and did not have very many friends. I felt like I had to develop ways of getting the other students, specifically the girls to like me and overcome my self-esteem problems. I never felt that my brothers had the same problems; I was that "nappy-headed" ugly boy of the family. This droves me to develop my basketball skills, to get the students to like me and impress the girls.

My father had always reminded me of how different I was than my brothers. I remember one Easter; my father took us to town to buy Easter suits. This store had suits hanging in the window for seven dollars and fifty cents. We went in the store, and my father told the clerk that he needed suits for the boys. When he referred to me, he stated" This boy is rough on clothes and shoes. I need something rough for him."

My brothers all received very nice suits; I was given the brown suit that had been hanging in the window that had a sun-bleached area all over one side. It was discounted because of the discoloration. I was forced to wear this suit with steel-toes work shoes. This did not help my self-esteem. I never forgave my father, and it followed me throughout my life.

Chapter 4

Overcoming Low Self-Esteem

We had a very good basketball team at our school. We played on an outside red clay court. Other students who had gymnasiums talked about our clay court. The day of a game was very exciting time at Wrens High School. The players were very popular. We were allowed to skip class to prepare the court. We were not as fortunate as other schools to have gymnasiums to play in, but most of these teams, we would beat at home and in their own gym. Game day was exciting, the whole town would come to see us play.

Basketball became a great ego booster for me. I was well-known in the area for my basketball talent, earning the title "the Dribbling King." This made me very popular in high school, and I was considered a very good point guard. My team depended a great deal on me. I can recall the time when we had a big home coming game. The day of the game, I was trying to iron a crease in my pants on the stove pipe and accidentally burned my right forearm on the hot pipe. That day, I felt so important to the team when the coach and others came to my house to prepare my burned arm and to make sure I was going to be able to play. I was one of the highest scoring point guards in the area, and my team depended on me scoring late points. I was able to play and help our team win the game. I slowly developed good, strong self-esteem, and I felt better about myself and was not afraid to talk to girls. Basketball became a driving force in my life, and it helped me overcome low self-esteem.

THE NEWS AND FARMER / THE JEFFERSON REPORTER

1957 Wrens basketball team...

Basketball team:

Left to right: Odell, George, Annanah, Jasper Roosevelt, Herman, James

As a family, we were always driven by our economic situation, and were forced to overcome all odds. My mother expected us to excel in school and whatever we did. Even though we were poor and had to pick cotton every year until after Thanksgiving, we still were number one or number two in our class most of the time. My mother would insist that after picking cotton for about ten hours a day, that my brothers, sisters, and I obtain the assignment for that day and study for hours. When we did start school, the other students would ask how we were able to keep up with everyone else. Not even poverty could keep us from being the best, dressing the best we could and feeling as if we were the best in the school. This was because of our mother who's philosophy was that we should be the best we could be. Even though the clothes we wore had holes in them, she insisted that they be clean, with creases in the pants but neatly worn at all times. No one knew that our clothes were hand me down from the other brothers, or sister for the girls, or sometimes from White families that my mother worked for. The shoes had holes in the soles but was polished and shined on top, and ironically, we were usually voted the best dressed in our class. Mother felt that this created character and good self-esteem. This philosophy followed me throughout life and played a tremendous role in my development. "For it is not what's on the outside that make the man, but what's on the inside, that makes the man."

Chapter 5

The Family Structure

There is a total of eleven children in my family. Ten children from the first marriage and one from a second marriage. There were five boys and three girls born in Zebina, Georgia. My oldest brother did not complete the ninth grade. He became tired of my father's drinking problems and being abused by him. He joined the army and later moved to Philadelphia to live with relatives, and he worked hard and developed a very good life for himself and his family. He was killed in a manhole while working for the City of Philadelphia, Pennsylvania.

My father abused us in many ways, but I can remember when he would force the boys (three or four) to go with him almost every Saturday morning to Hill Top, a bar about ten miles from Wrens. Our job was to sit out in the car while he goes in the bar to drink alcohol with his friends all day. He would intermittently bring one of his friends out to show off his boys. This would go on until sometimes late at night. He would occasionally bring us a hot dog and a soda. We would beg him not to take us with him, but he would not listen to us. My father had a favorite son that he depended on for all the news and gossip regarding the other members of the family. We would hope that he would just take him and leave us at home, but he wanted all of us to go with him. We received so many beatings because my brother would tell everything that we did.

I also remember how we would usually have one chicken for dinner, and we would not get any of the chicken until my father got the pieces he wanted. He would eat most of the chicken and leave two or three pieces to be divided between seven or eight of us. Sometimes, you may end up with a chicken foot. There were many disadvantages for being members of a large family, one would be that you may not get anything to eat if you did not get to the table in time. Usually, the meat would be gone. Timing for food was very important in our family, first come first served. Even after school, we would rush home to get left over grits and other foods. I recall making grit sandwiches or sometimes tomato sandwiches. Many fights have been initiated over food between my brothers and me, and sometimes my sisters as well. These fights usually led to whipping later by my mother.

My oldest sister kept us in line when mother was at work. Sometimes the whipping that we got from her was worse than our mother's. our big sister would sometimes break up fights between my mother and father. My father would usually stay drunk from Friday through Sunday and would usually come home early Saturday or Sunday morning and start a fight with my mother, physically beating her, usually every week. my father would get all of us up to prepare food for him or to ask us questions about what had occurred during the day. There were times when my mother would be beaten so badly that she would wake us up and make all of us put clothes in a bag, and we would walk five miles in the middle of the night to our grandmother's home, where we would stay until it was safe to go back home. This would occur over and over again, and sometimes we would stay from one to two weeks.

My oldest sister became very upset and angry at my father. One night, when he attempted to beat my mother, my sister picked up a board with a nail in it and hit him in the forehead. This stopped him for a short period from beating my mother. My mother soon divorced my father and was left to raise all of us alone. I was about eleven or twelve years old when my father left and cannot remember ever seeing him again alive. We were all adamant about never becoming a alcoholic or the type of father that he was. One of my sisters developed very low self-esteem and was surrounded by the wrong people, became an alcoholic, married, and hung around alcoholics. We all tried hard to help her and to keep her from those who we felt were influencing her. In spite of all our efforts, she died of liver failure at an early age.

Throughout all of our problems and family turmoil, our mother insisted on us excelling in school. She would talk to the teacher and obtain all of our grades to make sure we were making good grades. She would also inquire about our conduct in school. If the teacher told her we had not been doing what we should have we knew we were going to get a whipping, even though the teacher may have already whipped us. The teacher had a very strong interest in making sure we learned and succeeded in what we wanted to do. I do not think that I would have graduated from high school without the help, motivation, and encouragement from some of the teachers. To have eleven children in the family, I feel like my mother had a very good record my sisters and brothers, who finished before me were number one or two in their classes. My mother had done her part, the rest was up to us. All the children, except one, finished high school and all, except four, received further education after graduating from high school. For a family of eleven children, this is a very good success record.

Chapter 6

After Parents' Divorce

Most children would be upset when their mother and father separate, but that was not the case with us. We were happy that our daddy would no longer be coming home in the middle of the night abusing my mother and us.

The financial situation did not change though; we continued to work hard in the fields to buy food, clothes, pay the mortgage and utility as usual. My father usually spent his money on alcohol and other things that he desired, so he was not much of a financial help. My mother divorced my father, and he moved to Florida. We were never contacted by our father again. He was a known alcoholic as long as I can remember. After he left, we survived by obtaining little jobs on the weekend cutting grass, doing janitorial work, and etc. One of my brothers obtained a job as a shoeshine boy at the White barber shop in town. He also worked at the Bell Telephone Company office, cleaning up every weekend. These were both good jobs, and my brother was able to help out a great deal. When he left for the air force, these jobs were passed down to one of us. We had a very good reputation in the area.

After my father left, my mother found herself with six boys and four girls to raise alone. She was determined to not let us be like many of the other boys in the area, who were drinking alcohol, partying, and whatever else they wanted to do. She was determined that we were going to graduate from high school and be "somebody one day." She insisted that we be home before the sun went down, and we had to go to church every Sunday, as well as Sunday school.

My mother was only five feet tall and weighed about one hundred pounds. But when she spoke to you, you knew she meant every word she said, and you never thought about going against her. She put fear in us; we were afraid to do anything wrong. She constantly reminded us of our name and what it meant to us in the community. When the Fullard's name was mentioned, people respected it. The name was responsible for jobs that we were able to obtain. My brothers and I were much larger than our mother, but this never mattered to her. We received whippings throughout our teenaged years. Through all of this, we were always reminded of how much she loved us and wanted us to finish high school and grow up to be somebody one day.

I remember friends partying every weekend, drinking alcohol and just having a good time while we were not allowed to even play ball in front of our house after the sun went down; however, we never considered leaving home. There had to be something else that made us feel so loved by our mother and each other; to dream of not being together was unthinkable. There were so many children dropping out of school, walking the streets, and getting into trouble, but the community looked up to us as role models in the church and school. As much as I hated the whipping and strict control, it made us grow up to be good citizens and good representatives for our family and community.

Several years after the divorce from my father, my mother remarried and had another son, making us a total of eleven children. This marriage did not last long; her husband was later killed, and my mother never married again. My youngest brother was very smart and was raised the same as the rest of us. He graduated from high school and college. My mother raised seven boys and four girls mostly by herself. None of us got into trouble, and during this time, this was quite an accomplishment.

What we were able to do, I have given credit to my mother so many times. I am sure that I would not have completed high school and would have gotten into trouble like many of my friends were doing at that time. I am also sure I would not be the father or the husband that I am. My desire was to do right, to be a devoted church member, and a strong desire to be the best mentor or role model as I could be. Those whippings, strict rules, along with a demand that we go to church each Sunday shaped the man I am today. Don't even think that we did not love our mother; we would do anything to help her.

I can remember one morning around ten o' clock, she developed a severe nosebleed. After trying everything we could to stop the bleeding, we decided to take her to the only doctor in town. This was a White doctor, who did not really want to take care of Blacks. We arrived at the office and went into the waiting area for Blacks— a space approximately six feet by nine feet in size. We were using a towel applying pressure to decrease the bleeding. The receptionist told us we would have to wait until all the White patients had been seen. Looking across the offices, it was a very nice and large waiting room with only a few White patients. I can remember us standing most of the time until approximately four thirty in the evening, then my mother was finally seen. I was about twelve years old at that time.

I remember saying to my mother that one day I'm going to be a doctor so that Black people won't have to suffer like this. I don't know how I could even dream of becoming a doctor considering our financial situation. I guess this was something that just came out, and this experience confirmed the need to obtain a good education and to be prepared for a possibility in the future.

Following graduating from high school, I was very confused. I, had no plans and did not know what I was going to do. There was no money for college, and my classmates were talking about where they were going after graduation. I was depressed, and this was very obvious to my teachers. When I was approached by one of them, who asked what I was going to do. My response was "I don't know." She knew my financial situation and asked if I want to go to college. My answer was "Yes, ma' am, I would love to go to college." I was also asked if I would like to work my way through college. I said, "Yes, ma'am. I am used to work, and I would do anything to go to college."

I was told of a college called Tuskegee, Institute in Tuskegee, Alabama. Tuskegee had a five- year work program where you could work and go to college at the same time. I readily accepted this idea, but I was told that I needed to have three hundred fifty dollars at the time of registration. I felt that I could accomplish this over the summer. I applied to Tuskegee Institute and was accepted. I told everyone I saw. I was so happy. And that summer, I worked at Fort, Gordon in Augusta, Georgia, an army base located about thirty-five miles from Wrens, Georgia. This meant transportation to and from work every day, which took part of my profit. I found myself in a very bad situation. I needed to raise $350 and needed clothes to wear. After all my expenses, I had saved only one hundred dollars.

That summer following graduation from high school was very depressing, and I was left with a dilemma of how I was going to come up with enough money to register at Tuskegee. All my hopes and dreams were about to be derailed. My mother had no money to give me. After a great deal of soul- searching, I finally decided to get a bus ticket to Tuskegee and pack the few pieces of clothes I had.

As I was packing my bag with three pairs of pants, one coat, and one pair of shoes that had holes in the sole, my mother asked me, "Boy, what do you think you are doing?"

I remember as if it was yesterday. I said, "I have enough money to get there and back, and I am going."

Chapter 7

The Tuskegee Trip

Arriving on the campus, I had mixed emotions. I was very happy, but, at the same time, very sad. I knew I only had about three days before the last day for registration. This was supposed to be a five-year work program, so I made some contacts with the dean's office. I was sent to John A. Andrew Hospital on campus for interview for a job. I was hired immediately, as a janitor, and was to start work the next day. I had forgotten that I had to have the first semester tuition before I could enroll. Now I am down to one day before the last day of registration.

This was a very sad and lonely day for me, watching the others register, and they all seem to be happy and having fun. I was so amazed at the cars they were driving and the clothes they were wearing, this made me a little jealous and envious of them.

The last days of registration, about one thirty in the afternoon, I received a call from the dean's office; and I did not know what to expect. I thought I was being sent home already. When I arrived in the dean's office, he told me that my mother had mortgaged her house and could only get ninety dollars, and she was wiring those ninety dollars to me. I cried just to know she would mortgage the family house for me to go to school. With the seventy- five dollars I had, this left me needing one $185 to have the $350 needed for registration. Later that same day, I received a call from my brother who was in the air force. He asked if I had enough money to register. I told him I needed $185 more, and that day, he wired me two hundred dollars. I was able to register and was the happiest person on campus. I am now a college student at Tuskegee Institute on the five- year work- study program. It was up to me to work in order to earn my tuition, and room and board.

I worked thirty- two hours per week as a janitor at John A. Andrew Hospital and took at least twelve credit hours per semester. I took my job as a janitor very serious. I knew this was the only way I could go to college and change my economic situation. I shined the floor so good that the hospital manager would bring visitors to see me buff the floor. I was determined that I would not ever ask my mother or any other relative to send me any more money. My mother did, however, voluntarily send me twenty dollars during the five years I was at Tuskegee. Knowing the condition back home, I did not expect her to send me money.

Working at John A. Andrew Hospital was a good job, but it only paid in vouchers for tuition and boarding. There was no money for personal items or money for a Coke or snacks. I took on jobs cutting grass on Saturdays and Sundays, to earn extra money to spend, but there was no money for shoes or clothes. I wore the same pants and jacket and shoes with holes in the soles to everything I attended. Those were the same clothes that I had brought initially from home. Vesper service was required at Tuskegee for all students every Sunday. I wore the same coat, pants, and shoes to every Vesper service, and the other students made fun of me. They were talking about my shoes with holes in the soles and about me wearing the same jacket every Sunday. I soon became embarrassed and stopped going to Vesper service. After several misses, I was called to the dean's office. He asked me if I knew that I could be sent home for not attending Vesper service, and at that moment, I started to cry and stated that I had to wear the same clothes to Vesper and that the other students were making fun of me. The dean put his arms around me and reached in his jacket and gave me fifty dollars and told me to go across the street, and buy a coat, pants, and shoes. After that, I did not miss Vesper service again.

One of the hardest things for me was having a roommate who had a new convertible car and a closet full of clothes and did not have to work. I soon learned that sometimes having more can be negative; my roommate did not make it through his freshman year. I learned that having less and working hard to accomplish what you want makes you appreciate it more, and it means more to you. My self-esteem soon improved, and I was not ashamed of my poverty background. I held my head up and decided nothing was going to stop me from obtaining what I wanted.

Working at John A. Andrew Hospital was a blessing to me in so many ways. My supervisor was a very caring and loving person who was not only interested in me working but also getting a good education. They had a family type of relationship among the workers and the supervisor. She told me that whatever the job, do it as well as you can. She was just like a mother to me and to the other students; she invited us to dinner, and we did odd jobs like cutting her grass and helping her around her house. I took great pride in my work of five years.

Working there, I was able to meet a young man named John, who became a very good friend. He and I became very close as the years passed. We both were janitors, and I learned later that he was from the same area in Alabama as my girlfriend. We worked the night shift and formed a singing group harmonizing with the other janitors. We would practice in the basement each night after work and were together most of the time, and we made our work fun and would play jokes on each other. John was a "talker," even when he was eating. One day at lunch with my girlfriend and two other nurses, while he was talking, knowing that he would first sprinkle salt on his food without tasting it, I switched his salt with the pepper. He loaded his food with pepper and never stopped talking.

John A. Andrew Hospital was a neat experience for me; the janitors did a little of everything as needed.

I remember one day; the ambulance driver did not show up for work. A student on campus became ill and called for ambulance transportation. I had never driven a car as our family never owned a car. The hospital manager demanded that I go and pick up the student ASAP. I was the only person there to do this, and before I could tell him that I could not drive, he was gone. So I had to do it. I got in the ambulance and finally figured out how to crank it up then got it in the right gear. I took off going across the street, one side to the other. Finally,

I arrived at the dormitory, picked up the student, and headed back to the emergency room, again, going from side to side. The student was demanding that I let her walk to the ER. We finally made it back safely. That was the beginning of my learning to drive. The hospital manager demanded that I learn to drive and get my license. This news spread all over campus, and no one wanted me to pick them up again. My friend John did not let me forget that experience.

I met my wife, Patricia a very attractive and smart nurse working at the hospital. She was a nurse in the neo natal nursery on the three-to- eleven shift at the hospital. It was love at first sight for me, but it took work to gain her interest. Patricia was such an attractive young lady that I did not think I had a chance of dating her. I had noticed her many times at the hospital but had not approached her.

But in December 1960, John A. Andrew Hospital had an annual Christmas party for the staff during working hours, so the staff had to take turns. It was about ten thirty in the evening before she arrived at the Christmas party; she arrived wearing her crisp- white uniform. First, she danced with the head of pediatrics, later with the head of the obstetrics. Then I asked her to dance, and she agreed. It was a slow dance. She told me later that she was so mad because it was a slow dance, and it seemed as if I just stood in one place. We did dance a fast dance before she returned to duty. She was staying at Dorothy Hall Guest house on campus. I stayed and walked her home that night and each night thereafter. We both ate at the hospital cafeteria, all three meals. She moved from Dorothy Hall to Olivia Davidson Hall. I still continued to walk her home every night.

As we became good friends, we shared our stories and found out that we both had experienced similar backgrounds, and we had a lot in common. We both came from very small country towns from the South. She was from Hartselle, Alabama, and I was from Wrens, Georgia. We had been dating for less than a year when I decided that she was the person I wanted to marry, and I finally got enough nerve to ask her. And she said yes. We had not met each other's families because I did not have a car and did not have money to lease a car. A very close friend from my hometown agreed to let me borrow his car. We took our first trip home to my family. Then we went to her hometown. I stayed at my friend John's house that weekend. I had already written a letter to her mother and father, telling them how I felt about their daughter and that I wanted to marry her. Her father was a minister and gave his permission to marry his daughter. Her mother was a very kind and loving person. I felt like I had made the right decision.

Chapter 8

The Wedding

We returned to Tuskegee to plan our wedding that was to take place in a few months. I received a preceptorship that summer at North Carolina, A and T. College, Greensboro, North Carolina, on "The Effect of Radiation on the Cells." Part of my stipend was used to buy a wedding set for our engagement. I was twenty-two years old, and she was twenty. We both were poor, but she wanted a church wedding. Her grandfather and father were ministers, and it was decided that her father would marry us; and her oldest sister would do all the planning in Hartselle. I had spent all of my money on the rings, so I did not have money for the license. I had to borrow the money from my fiancée to pay for the license.

My mother lived in Wrens, Georgia, approximately 350 miles from Hartselle, Alabama. I caught the bus and went home and drove my mother to Hartselle in her car to our wedding. I stayed two houses away, with my friend John, and my mother stayed at her parents' home. The week of our wedding, her father had a stroke and was not able to officiate the wedding. Her grandfather, who was a minister, married us. Her uncle walked her down the aisle. It was a beautiful church wedding, and the reception was at the parsonage. My bride wore a beautiful white ankle length dress, beautiful jewelry, white shoes, and a white veil. Three of her sisters were brides' maids, and her best friend and classmate was her maid of honor. I wore a black suit and black bow tie with black shoes with holes in the sole but shining on top. I thought I had made it because I did not think I would have to kneel down in front of the audience. Her grandfather had us kneel down at the altar for prayer, and someone took a picture of me kneeling with the holes in my shoes. This picture has followed me until this day. We were married on September 2, 1962.

After the wedding and reception, I drove my mother's car to a nearby town called Huntsville, Alabama, to the Gladys Jane Motel. It was the nearest Black motel. We stayed that night, came back the next day, picked up my mother at my now in-laws' home; we also picked up our shower and wedding gifts that we received and took them back to Tuskegee. I do not remember if I drove my mother home, or she drove herself home. But we went back to Tuskegee; I continued to work as a janitor to pay my tuition, to finish my senior year, and for her to continue working at John A. Andrew hospital. We stayed with friends for a few weeks (she was a registered nurse, and he was an engineer at the Veterans Hospital) until we were able to move in our one- bedroom apartment by the post office and was in walking distance to the campus and the grocery store. I remember we would walk to the grocery store once a month to get groceries which would last for the month.

I graduated from Tuskegee Institute on May 1963 with a Bachelor of Science degree in biology. During my last year of undergraduate school, my wife became pregnant. This was a very rough time for us. We were in a lot of debt and had no means of transportation; I was very concerned about how I would get her to the hospital at the time when she would go into labor. We had a very close friend that lived close by. I asked if I could borrow his car when my wife went into to labor, and he agreed. I did not know it was a stick shift. When she started having labor pains, we both panicked. I ran over to pick up the car and found out it was a stick- shift transmission. After picking up my wife, I ran in a ditch. With help, I was able to get out the ditch, and we made it to the hospital, and our first son arrived on June 28, 1963, at two fifty-five in the morning and weighed five pounds and fourteen ounces.

After receiving my Bachelor of Science degree in biology with a minor in chemistry, I applied for a teaching position near my hometown, Wrens, Georgia. I was offered a teaching job for three thousand dollars per year. We were so happy and felt like this was my big opportunity. I accepted the position and started making plans to move back to Georgia. Mother was very happy to know that her son was going to be a teacher in Wrens. This was considered one of the highest positions that a Black person had ever held in Wrens. The word got around in town that the poor Black boy from Wrens had graduated from Tuskegee Institute and was returning to teach science at Wrens High School. I still remember that trip to Wrens that summer with my wife and my first baby who was only a few weeks old. We had rented a small trailer that we pulled behind our '59 Ford. This was a big thing for my family and me.

As soon as we arrived in Wrens, I received a call from someone who informed me of a job in Denton, Maryland, that was paying three thousand five hundred dollars per year. This was exciting for someone who had not been able to take care of his family, working years as a janitor for vouchers that could only be used for tuitions and room and board. All I could think of was that I would be able to take care of my family. Many were very disappointed with my decision to go to Denton, but I felt this was the right thing for us to do at this time.

Chapter 9

Denton, Maryland

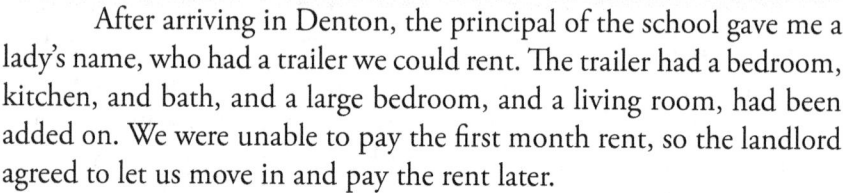

After arriving in Denton, the principal of the school gave me a lady's name, who had a trailer we could rent. The trailer had a bedroom, kitchen, and bath, and a large bedroom, and a living room, had been added on. We were unable to pay the first month rent, so the landlord agreed to let us move in and pay the rent later.

After arriving, we had to buy food, diapers, milk for our six-week- old baby. This was a big problem initially; we had to budget every penny in order to make it through the first month. I guess I had not thought about the difference in the cost of living in Maryland as opposed to Wrens, Georgia. Staying in Wrens would have been the best economical decision, but now that we are here, we had to make the best of it.

The first meeting at the school, the new teachers were told how the different classes were reorganized. Apparently, the students had been given a national standardized test, and the score on the test determined whether they were in class A, B, C, or D. Being new to teaching, I was not aware of how this worked. I was later informed by the students that the A and B classes were students who make As and Bs, and these were students that would go to college. The students in classes C and D were not college material but may qualify for vocational school. This was later confirmed by other teachers. I became very upset that one examination could have such devastating effect on these students' lives. The day of the examination could have been a day when the student did not feel well or had not eaten or were upset about something. I set out to prove them wrong and change the self-esteem and future lives of these students.

I informed the students that I never believed in giving students grades that they did not earn, but I would stay after school and during lunch time to help them understand the material and improve their grades and knowledge of the material. I was determined to change the way things had always been done. I began to notice a change in some of the students in group C and D. Some began to make As and Bs. This was the group that I focused on in terms of spending extra time with them. Some of the students in group A's and B's grades decreased; unfortunately, some of these students had been told that they were A and B students and could not receive C and D grades, and the C and D group felt that they could not receive A and B grades.

In one of my classes, there was a very smart student who informed me that we were related. I was not aware of any relatives in Maryland. After school that day, he indicated that his mother and my mother were half-sisters, and I contacted my mother who also confirmed it. This was very good news since I did not know anyone in the area. I talked to his mother and brothers who asked me if we needed anything. I learned that they owned a two-hundred-acre produce farm, and they offered to bring us vegetables and meat. This was such a big blessing for us because we were barely surviving on my salary. My wife later obtained a job as an LPN at a nearby hospital but later developed a thyroid disorder that required surgery. While she was in the hospital, my newly discovered relatives were very helpful in taking care of our son for six weeks so that I could work. I don't know what I would have done if it had not been for my new relatives. They were a lifesaver for my family during the time I spent in Denton, Maryland.

Moving to Denton, Maryland, was full of surprises for my family and me. I remember experiencing my first snow. I had never driven in snow before. And one morning on my way to work, there must have been about three inches of snow on the highway. I was sliding all across the highway and ran into the porch and mailbox of a little White lady's house, and the porch and mailbox was destroyed. As a Black boy from the South, I was very afraid of what could happen.

I knocked on the door and said to the lady who answered the door, "I am sorry, I ran into your porch and mailbox…"

And before I could finish, she said, "Are you the new teacher at Lockerman High School?"

I answered, "Yes, ma'am."

As I was having flash backs from the South, she spoke up and said, "Go on to school, and when you finish stop back by."

I worried that whole day about what was going to happen. I knew I could not afford to pay for the damages. I stopped by after school, and to my surprise, the porch and the mailbox was repaired. I knocked on the door and asked her how much I owed her, and she said nothing; "Everything has been repaired." I guess it was at this point that I realized I was in Maryland and not in Georgia.

After this experience, I was beginning to settle down and adjust to my new town. I felt good about what I had been able to accomplish with the students. I felt I had made an impact on several of the students' lives. I had observed students becoming more interested in learning and more motivated and developed better self- esteem; however, I was told that at the end of the year, there would be a staff meeting to discuss the success of the year. I soon learned the real reason for this meeting; the principal would discuss the students' grades and decide whether or not grades received were correct. At this meeting, when he got to my students, I was told that some of the students in the C and D group had received A and B grades and that some of the students in the A and B groups had received Cs and Ds, and I was told these grades need to be changed. I informed him that these were the grades that these students had earned and worked hard for, and I would not change the grades. I resigned from the staff following the meeting.

Following my resignation, I made contact with a professor at Tuskegee Institute who informed me that there was a grant supported position for a masters in zoology. I applied and was accepted to start a master's program in September 1964. The grant provided tuition and a stipend. I was very happy, but I had a big dilemma— I had no income during the summer months. So, I applied to Morgan State College in Maryland for a summer program that paid a stipend, and I was accepted to this program.

My wife and I decided that she and the baby would go back to Tuskegee for the summer and await my return after the summer program at Morgan State. A very close friend and her husband agreed to let my wife and baby stay with them until I return to work on my master's degree. This was the first time we had been away from each other since our marriage. My wife has always been supportive and understanding about anything I wanted to do. She applied to and was employed at the Veterans Administration Hospital at Tuskegee, Alabama. Every success depends on an opportunity, and without the right situation, you will not be able to take advantage of the opportunities that are presented to you. This is definitely true as it relates to the role my wife has always played in everything that I have accomplished. She was the "bread winner" in the home while I attended school, and she deserves at least half of whatever I have accomplished. Without her, none of this would have been possible.

Chapter 10

Returned to Tuskegee for Graduate School

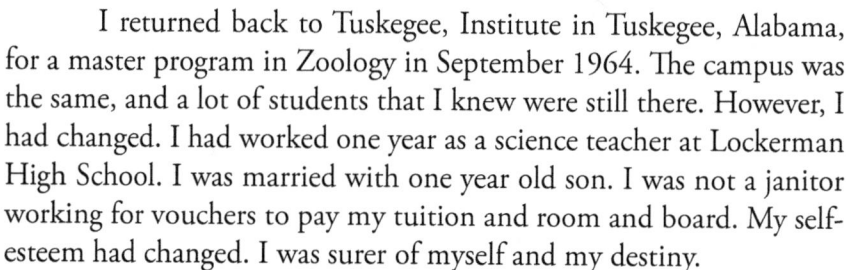

I returned back to Tuskegee, Institute in Tuskegee, Alabama, for a master program in Zoology in September 1964. The campus was the same, and a lot of students that I knew were still there. However, I had changed. I had worked one year as a science teacher at Lockerman High School. I was married with one year old son. I was not a janitor working for vouchers to pay my tuition and room and board. My self-esteem had changed. I was surer of myself and my destiny.

I was given a grant to cover my tuition and a stipend to help with my living expenses. We were able to move into "the projects" near campus. My wife's sister was able to come and stay with us and take care of the baby while my wife worked at Veterans Administration Hospital in Tuskegee. I was able to go to school, and my sister- in-law was able to go to business school at night. Everything fell into place for my family and I. This allowed me to concentrate on school.

My professor was a very caring and dedicated person whom I had the opportunity to take several courses with and to assist in his lab. He allowed me to choose a research project for my master thesis. I chose to study "The Effect of Radiation on the Development of Chicken Embryos." I fell in love with this project and spent lots of time studying radiation, and its effect on animal cells and tissues. My project required many dozens of fertilized eggs that were incubated and allowed to grow for various numbers of weeks before analyzing the effects of the radiation. There were many controls that had no radiation exposure. At the end, we had a small chicken farm. I still own the upright freeze that I purchased in 1964 to keep the unexposed chickens that we were able to eat.

My graduate experience was very rewarding to me; it gave me the opportunity to teach general biology and zoology to a large freshman class, as many as two hundred to three hundred students. Maybe my experience at Lockerman high school helped me prepare for this experience. I received a great review from the students. I have always loved teaching and watching students learn, and understanding the material was a great feeling. I believe my ability to teach in such a way that students can learn the material evolved out of my years in undergraduate school, having to work thirty- two hours per week, and taking eleven to twelve credits. I had to find ways to simplify materials so that I could understand it within the time I had to study. I also assisted my professor with the labs for anatomy and physiology, which made me feel like one of the professors at Tuskegee.

During my master's year, I took courses from the school of Veterinary Medicine at Tuskegee. Those courses included histology and embryology and anatomy. Tuskegee School of Veterinary Medicine was ranked number three in the country. This experience was very helpful to me in relation to my research project. Those courses were not easy. I worked very hard. At that time, I got a little taste of what medicine would be like. I still remember the promise I had made to my mother, that one day I would be a doctor. These dreams made me work just that much harder.

During undergraduate school, I used to watch pledgees every year and wished I could pledge. My work schedule and a lack of the money required prevented me from pledging. Now again, these thoughts haunted me. I decided to pledge Kappa Alpha Psi Fraternity on my graduate year at Tuskegee. Although I enjoyed being a Kappa, I felt that pledging as a graduate student was not the same as being an undergraduate. I was married and had a son, and everyone knew this. I didn't get the same response from the girls as the other pledges, but this was something I could cross off my bucket list. I was proud of what

I had accomplished. Lots of people will never understand this, but to finally obtain something that you felt you could never have, that made me feel so good.

During the early parts of my graduate year, my wife became pregnant with our second child. This put a little strain on our financial situation; she had to take off work for short periods. We had our second son on March 1, 1966; he weighed six pounds and fifteen ounces. We did survive my graduate school year, and I received my master's degree in zoology on May 1966. I felt so good about this degree. For a young Black man who had nothing and no chance of getting out of a small country town, I have succeeded in obtaining a bachelor's and master's degree. This was for all the poor children who have very little economic support. You too can make it if you do not let your limitations limit you.

It seems as if God was testing us. For every year that I received a degree, we would have a baby. This was a blessing from God.

At the time when my second son was born, we were living in a two- bedroom project apartment. My oldest son was able to have his first puppy. He loved that puppy and would carry the puppy around by his neck. The puppy finally died, and we decided that this would be his last puppy.

We were later forced to look for a larger home that would allow my wife's sister to live with us and help take care of my two boys while my wife worked, and I attended school. My sister- in- law was also able to attend business school at night. We moved to a brick house with three bedrooms and much more space for the boys to play. One day before going to school, my sister- in-law saw a snake in the yard. I have always been afraid of snakes but realized that my oldest son would pick up any animals without fear. I had to do something before going to school. My wife's father was a hunter, and after he passed, she received his old shotgun that we had never used and did not know how to use. I raised the window, loaded the gun, and shot at the snake. The shot was not even close to the snake, the snake went slowly into the wooded area behind the house. I had blood all over my chin, and I had to go to school with a large bandage on my chin, which created questions and forced me to explain the snake story over and over.

Chapter 11

Tent City, Tuskegee Connection

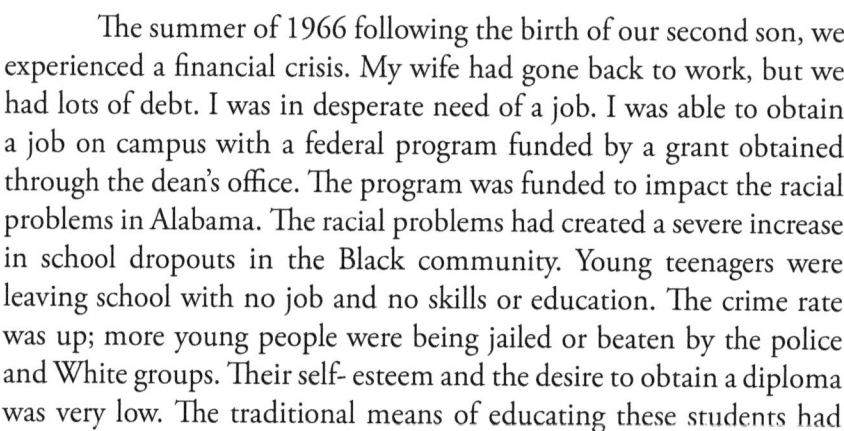

The summer of 1966 following the birth of our second son, we experienced a financial crisis. My wife had gone back to work, but we had lots of debt. I was in desperate need of a job. I was able to obtain a job on campus with a federal program funded by a grant obtained through the dean's office. The program was funded to impact the racial problems in Alabama. The racial problems had created a severe increase in school dropouts in the Black community. Young teenagers were leaving school with no job and no skills or education. The crime rate was up; more young people were being jailed or beaten by the police and White groups. Their self- esteem and the desire to obtain a diploma was very low. The traditional means of educating these students had failed.

The Tuskegee program was designed to utilize nontraditional means of reaching and motivating these young school dropouts. I was hired as one of the supervisors of the thirteen counties in Alabama. Many young White students from the northern states volunteered to help solve the problems across the South. One of the White volunteers was assigned to transport me to and from the county. This was not tolerated in the South; the KKK were active in Alabama. I remember one day on the way back from the county, I needed to use the bathroom, and there was no place to stop for Blacks. I asked the White young lady who was driving to stop beside the road, so I could go into the woods to urinate. Just as I had gotten into the wooded area, I saw a light and someone said, "There is a colored boy. Let's get him." I managed to get back in the car, and we pulled away before getting caught. After that experience, I requested that the person chosen to drive me to and from the counties in Alabama to be Black or at least a White man.

The Tuskegee program had a tremendous effect on my life. It taught me so much about how to teach and motivate young Black students who had no self- esteem or desire to learn. Traditional approach to this problem had failed, leaving a large number of young teenagers to feel that they could not learn and would not go to college or vocational school. The Tent City Project was designed specifically to reach those students who had dropped out of school and had no hope. Tents were set up in thirteen counties, and the targeted students were recruited, brought in the tents, given food to eat, interviewed to determine where each student's education level was. They were placed in groups according to their level of education. The teachers were told to develop lesson plans that best fit each group's level of understanding or education.

The objectives were to teach each student and not to focus on age or the level of education that should correspond with that age. If the objective is to teach algebra, then you must make sure all the students know basic math, adding, subtraction, multiplication, division, etc. before trying to teach what a+b is. A number of students had problem reading but loved comic books. They were encouraged to bring their comic books and read them and later report on what they had read; and their interest in reading increased, and they felt also better about participating in discussions. This program required the teacher to make several lesson plans, which required teacher assistants to help bring all the students to the same level. The teaching concept was very successful. Most of the students received their diploma and went on to college, to become doctors, lawyers, teachers, nurses, etc. I believe that my experience with this program contributed to my ability to teach students of all backgrounds and levels of education. I became known for my ability to teach with focus on the individual student and not on completing a book or certain amount of material.

Chapter 12

Stillman College

Following graduation, with a Master of Science degree, I accepted a job at Stillman College in Tuscaloosa, Alabama. I had fallen in love with Tuskegee and would like to have stayed there, but there were no jobs available. I met a friend who was teaching at a Stillman College in Tuscaloosa, Alabama. He informed me that he was taking another position at a larger college, and his position would be available. I applied and was accepted to teach biology, zoology, and general science. The job paid six thousand dollars per year. That's almost twice as much as I had made in Denton, Maryland. My wife and I were so excited; she was able to transfer from Veterans Hospital in Tuskegee, Alabama, to the Veterans Hospital in Tuscaloosa, Alabama, which was a psychiatric hospital. Stillman College is a Presbyterian college at that time with 90 percent of the faculty being Caucasian, and the student body was 90 percent Black. At first, I was a little concerned about possible racial issues. After talking to several students, my concern was eliminated. The faculty was very dedicated and committed. My first visit to Stillman College was very impressive, and I was sold. The students were very eager to learn. I felt like I would be back doing what I had done at Tuskegee. I was very interested in making sure that the students understood and learned the material and not just completing a course.

After the first year at Stillman College, several students asked why they couldn't obtain a degree that would allow them to go into professions other than teaching. At that time, I did not realize that after graduation, these students were mostly restricted to teaching. Several students were interested in nursing, dental, and the medical professions. I spent time looking for the curriculum that we were offering the students and came to the same conclusion as many of the students had. Having an interest in medicine as well got me interested in trying to do something about this problem. This was my chance to help these students realize their dream in life.

I talked to the other instructors about this problem, and I was so surprised that they had some interests and concerns about this as well. I gathered information from the University of Alabama School of Medicine and put together a proposal to be presented to the president and other administrative staff. The proposal was approved by the executive board and president with pending details of who would teach specific courses; this was worked out with the biology and science teachers. I volunteered to teach anatomy and physiology, embryology and histology. The physics and chemistry teachers covered those specialty areas. The materials taught in each specialty area were upgraded to make sure the students would have adequate credits for the requirement for pre-med. school, nursing, and other health care professions. I was very happy about the outcome of this program. Many students have graduated and have gone on to medicine, nursing, and many other healthcare professions. Later, I was appointed chairman of the department of biology and co chairman of the division of arts and science. This was one of my greatest and happiest experiences at Stillman College.

In 1967, while I was at Stillman College, I heard that three of my brothers were going to Florida to check on my father, whom I had not seen for many years. They were going to try to bring him to Philadelphia, but he refused to leave Florida. Weeks later, my brothers received a call to come back and pick him up because he had no place to live, and he was completely blind. Two of my brothers went back to Florida to pick him up and carried him to Philadelphia. He was placed in a government supported apartment, and they were also able to get him in a school for the blind. As the story goes, he and a female friend was arguing over money, and he slapped her. She hit him in the head with a two- by- four board. He was taken to the hospital and later died. I was notified in Tuscaloosa, Alabama, of his passing. The funeral was the first time I had seen him since the divorce from my mother. Unfortunately, no one has a picture of him. My children and grandchildren have asked about a picture of him many times. I am glad my brothers were able to forgive him and tried to help him before he died.

Chapter 13

The Move to Madison, Wisconsin, "PhD Program"

After my second year at Stillman College, the Ford Foundation was offering small colleges an opportunity to upgrade their faculties. I was offered an opportunity to work on a PhD in anatomy and physiology with all expenses paid. I applied to the University of Wisconsin in Madison, Wisconsin, and was accepted.

There were a few obstacles that I had to overcome, such as the house we had purchased in Tuscaloosa, Alabama, was only two years old. However, we were able to lease the house to two teachers and were planning to return to this house after I completed my Ph.D. Being accepted to the University of Wisconsin with expenses paid was another blessing I could not have dreamed of, and in the fall of 1968, we moved to Madison, Wisconsin. We were able to live in the graduate students with children apartments called Eagle Heights, not too far from the Veterans Administration Hospital. My wife was able to transfer from the Veterans Administration in Tuscaloosa, Alabama, to the VA in Madison, Wisconsin. Initially, her assignment was a floater on the three- to- eleven shifts in the medical intensive care unit or the surgical intensive care unit.

The other families in the apartments where we lived were very nice; they were always willing to help each other with babysitting. Because we were all struggling, we also had a baby-sitting pool; we had cards that were used (hourly, one- half hour, and fifteen minutes). If you needed babysitting for any length of time, you paid with cards like money. Example, if you were gone two hours and a half for shopping to buy groceries, ball games, or activities on campus, when you return home, you would pay the sitter two one- dollar cards and one- half-hour cards.

My wife worked 3:00 to 11:00 or 11:00 to 7:00 a.m., so I could go to school during the day, and I would keep the boys at night. After they would go to bed, I would study at home. This worked out very well.

Wisconsin was very cold, something that we had to adjust to. There were times when my wife had to walk to and from work in the ice and snow. The boys loved playing in the snow and sliding on the ice. Our oldest son joined the hockey team at school. I had very little free time concentrating on studying and watching the boys. I became very good at cooking pork and beans and wieners. My children still talk about this today. We had to make lots of adjustments in the transition from the South to Wisconsin.

I was very excited about getting started on my PhD program. During my first year at Wisconsin, we would receive many calls about the condition of our house we left in Tuscaloosa, Alabama. The tenants that we had so much trust in had destroyed the house. They were constantly calling about things that needed repaired. We had to obtain a realtor to sell the house.

Although working on a PhD in anatomy was a big challenge for me, I really enjoyed working with my professor and assisting with teaching the lab for histology and embryology to medical students. I never forgot about my dream to go to medical school. I had a strong background in histology and embryology during my master's degree training at Tuskegee.

The PhD research project included minor surgery on rats, working with my professor. I was instructed to do an intestinal bypass surgical procedure on rats to study the effects on absorption. I embraced this challenge, and my desire to become a medical doctor grew more and more each day. I had done similar projects for my master's degree at Tuskegee, studying "The Effect of X-Irradiation on the Embryological Development in the Chicks." There I had to radiate eggs and later study the histological effects of radiation on the cells of various organs of the chicken. It was because of my strong desire to become a medical doctor and my experiences with my professor's project that made me pursue this opportunity to apply to medical school at the University of Wisconsin.

Other events that led to my decision was one night, about one o'clock in the morning, I had just left the lab, and I heard a big loud noise. After arriving at home, I heard that someone had bombed the pharmacy building across from my lab, and the windows were blown out in the lab where I had been working. This was during the time when students were protesting against the Vietnam war, and the pharmacy department was involved in research that supported the war. A great deal of my research project was affected, and I was discouraged. I later met with my professor and told him that I have always wanted to be a medical doctor and that I wanted to apply to medical school. He supported the decision and recommended me to the school of medicine. At that time, I had completed almost all my course work for a PhD in anatomy. I applied and was accepted to the school of medicine at the University of Wisconsin, Madison Campus.

The year 1970 was a very special year for me. Having to struggle with my decision to switch over from a PhD program to medicine was a big step. But more importantly, the birth of our little girl on May 27, 1970, at nine forty- two in the morning; she weighed six pounds and one-half ounces. She was delivered at St. Mary's Hospital, Madison, Wisconsin, and was a blessing to us. I had predicted after we got married that we would have two boys first then a girl; to have this come true was another sign from God that I was doing the right thing.

At the time of the delivery, I remember that my wife had picked out a name that I could not remember, pronounce, nor spell. I finally convinced her to change her name to something I could remember and spell. She agreed, and we chose my mother's first name and her mother's first name and put it together.

With my aspirations to become a doctor, I had decided to deliver my daughter. After I almost passed out, I was taken out of the delivery room. Following the birth of my daughter, we felt that our family was complete. I was very concerned about the extra burden that would be on my wife, having to take care of three children and work full time while I attended medical school. Having her sister living with us and helping with the children was such a blessing, and my mother-in-law would come up often to help with the children.

Chapter 14

Medical School

Attending medical school was my dream and aspiration since early childhood. I had no idea of the road I would travel to get to this point. Sometimes, you have to take a much more difficult path to reach your goal. There were many obstacles along the way that would normally cause one to give up and seek another path.

Now I find myself in medical school at the University of Wisconsin, one of the most prestigious medical schools that had not had a good reputation for admitting Black students. I was the only Black student in my class; this itself was a very fascinating phenomenon. I stood out in the classroom like a "sore thumb." I couldn't miss a class for I would be readily missed. Coming from the South, I anticipated a racial battle, and I was often asked questions by my professors that were meant to embarrass me or to show that I did not belong there. Many times, I would go home defeated and discouraged, but I was determined not to allow this to cause me to give up. I have faced racism all my life and have learned how to deal with it.

The experience I obtained during my master's and PhD courses prepared me for courses in anatomy, histology, and embryology. I was much better prepared in these areas than most of the other students, many who would seek my help in these areas. This gave validation to me that I was at the right place and that I could compete with any of the other students there. I was constantly reminded of my conversation with my mother at the age of eleven, when she almost bled to death when a White doctor refused to see her until all of the White patients had been seen. This is what motivated me and forced me to go through all the turmoil and pain that it took to get to this point. I knew that I could not turn around now. I had already experienced all of the racial pressure that anyone could ever expect, and medical school would only be another chapter that I had to experience. I was prepared for the worse that the professors and students could bring. I just needed to concentrate on studying and learning the massive amount of information and materials that would be given to me. Being the only Black student in the class carried a great disadvantage. I did not have anyone to study with and discuss ideals with. It was a lesson learned early, so I did not waste time focusing on it.

I remember doing the anatomy course; we had to work in groups to dissect the cadaver, and no one would choose me to be a part of their group. The professor had to assign me to a group. My background in anatomy soon made my group very popular, and the students would come around asking questions and sometimes questions with racial over tones, about the difference in anatomical parts between Whites and Blacks. My cadaver was a Black male that was very muscular, which made it easier to dissect out the muscles. I was prepared for the racial questions about why Blacks had more muscles, and why they were more athletic and could run faster and jump higher than Whites. This anatomy course taught me a lot about how others would treat me later and throughout medical school.

I had to develop good study habits and techniques in order to be able to learn lots of detailed information, not only to do well on examinations but also to be able to answer detailed questions that I would be expected to answer in the presence of the other students before they had an opportunity to answer. I started using note cards that I would carry with me everywhere I went and every chance I got; I would pull the cards out and flip through them. This was very helpful in learning lots of detailed- type information. These cards served as my study partner, and I was usually prepared for questions from the professor.

This soon took the focus off of me in class. I learned early that I would have to study hard to compete with students who always had everything they needed to prepare them for this experience. What made this more difficult for me was having to take care of two boys, ages five and two years old. My wife worked evenings or night shifts at the VA Hospital. I would have to take care of the children while my wife worked, which made it hard to study at home until they had gone to sleep. I would go to the library for a few hours after classes and my wife's days off and weekends. I would sometimes study in the student union where I could smoke my pipe. At that time, I thought it was a very cool thing to do until once, while I was studying in the student union, there was a very lovely young lady that would always sit in front of me and would smile when I would light up my pipe. One day, when I lit up my pipe, she reached into her bag, pulled out a pipe, and lit it. After that, I did not think it was cool to smoke, and with my wife complaining about me smoking at home, I soon stopped smoking my pipe. That was the first time I had seen a lady smoke a pipe, and I did not think it was cool.

Studying in the library and the student union was sometimes very distracting; at times, a student may run though the library naked. Streaking on campus was popular at that time. Outside of the student union was a lake that was frozen most of the time. During the winter and spring, students would drive cars, do tricks, and go ice fishing on the lake. Wisconsin was very cold, and coming from the South, I was not prepared for the ice and snow. I soon learned that the clothes that I brought with me from the South were not going to work in Wisconsin. I remember those "long johns" that my mother would make us wear to school, I would go to the bathroom and take them off at school and put them back on before going home to keep from getting a whipping. I called my mother and asked her to send me some long johns to wear. She reminded me that I never wanted to wear them when I was home. I convinced her that I would definitely wear them in Wisconsin.

My first and second year in medical school was very difficult. Trying to be a father to my children and going to medical school, I had to adjust my schedule according to my wife's work schedule. My wife worked hard to provide for the family while I was in school. Sometimes, she had to walk to work in the ice and snow when I was unable to drive her to work. Living in Eagle Heights Apartments on campus was very good for graduate students. There were play areas for the children and space for a garden if desired. These apartments were for families, and families were very supportive of each other and would help with childcare when necessary.

After the first half of the first year in medical school, I recognized the need for more Black students. I remembered a very close friend that took my position at Stillman College when I came to Wisconsin. He and I had been talking, and I realized that he was interested and would be an excellent choice to apply to medical school. He applied and was accepted, and I was very happy to have someone that I could trust as a friend and someone who had some of the same experiences that I had. He also had concerns about the need for Black physicians in the Black community. There were former students at Stillman College who had completed the premed program that I had initiated at Stillman College, who were also excellent potential candidates for medical school. I encouraged them to apply, and they were also accepted. This made me very proud to know that someone who I had taught and had completed the pre-med program that I initiated was accepted to medical school at the University of Wisconsin.

I do not want to give the impression that medical school was easy; it took all of my time and concentration on studying, and I had very little time for a social life. Getting to this point and moving forward was a big challenge for me. I was glad to have another Black student to study with and to discuss various problems, and in later years, many other Black students were admitted to medical school at the University of Wisconsin.

This was not easy for me. Coming from Wrens, Georgia, I had very little exposure to scientific equipment and instruments. This was a big void in my experience. I had to spend so much of my time trying to fill this void. However, having a master's degree in zoology was very helpful. There was so much I had to learn that other students took for granted. I always had to work twice as hard as other students through undergraduate and graduate school and now also in medical school. This was a challenge for me that I have always faced, and now I find myself here at the University of Wisconsin in medical school. Initially, the only Black student in class with no one else to trust to confide in, and to study with. I had to learn early who to trust and who were my friends. I knew that the White students didn't like me.

I remember a Black female student who had all A's through high school and undergraduate school, who was in all the newspapers. All the Black students were so happy and were looking forward to meeting her. When she arrived on campus, she isolated herself from the Black students and associated only with the White students. She partied with them and sometimes studied with them but was naive and thought they were her friends. We tried to tell her that they could not be trusted. They would party late at night and stay up and study the rest of the night while she would go to sleep. At the time for examinations, she did not do well and did not pass the first year.

My second year in medical school was a tough year for me because the number of courses per semester were increased significantly. We had nine courses on the organ systems each semester, which meant that we had to take nine exams in one day. The day started at seven in the morning and lasted to six in the evening, with one hour for lunch. I did okay on all of the examinations except the test on the liver. The cut off was set by the professor one point above my name, and I did not pass the liver test. I was forced to repeat part of that semester. I always felt that the professor deliberately set the cut offline so that I would not pass the course. But I would not allow this to derail what I was determined to accomplish. This was another obstacle that I had to overcome, and after that, I was able to complete that second year in medical school.

The third year of medical school was the clinical year, which meant that we spent a lot of time in the hospital seeing patients and doing history and physicals exams. This turned out to be another challenge for me because many of the White patients did not want a Black student examining them. It was very hard to obtain a history and physical exam on most of the White patients that I was assigned to. So, I would try to get the Black patients; however, there were not very many Black people in Madison, Wisconsin. After evaluating the patients, I would have to present the patient to the attending physician and the other students. The attending physician would take advantage of every opportunity to show the other students that I was not smart enough to be in medical school. I always felt that I had to be twice as smart as the White students just to get a little credit. I do not believe that they were so concerned about me and wanted to make sure I understood everything, but when you are a part of a group of six students and most of the questions are directed to you, this did not make me feel that the attending physician was trying to be fair to me. I always felt targeted in most of the discussions, but this made me study just that much harder. I refused to be defeated.

During my fourth year, I was offered a preceptorship at Mount Sinai Hospital in Milwaukee, Wisconsin. This was a very good experience for me, and I was able to actually see patients in the office with one of the doctors there. The preceptorship lasted for two months. I would go back to Madison to see my family about every other weekend. There was a larger Black population in Milwaukee than in Madison. I am not sure that this was the reason I was encouraged to except this preceptorship, but it did allow me to see and examine more patients, most of which were Black.

The fourth year of medical school was much more relaxed, but you had to be on call for twenty-four- hour shifts. I had to do history and physical exams on all patients admitted from the emergency room and present them to the attending physician the next morning. This was my time to show him that I understood the material well and deserved to be a doctor along with the other medical students. Against all the odds, I still had to take the same national examination as the other students. I passed the test the first time, but a number of students had to repeat the examination before receiving the MD license.

At the end of the fourth year, you participate in a match system to determine where you would do your internship. My first choice was Kansas University Medical Center in Kansas City, Kansas; I matched my first pick and was accepted to Kansas Medical Center to do my internship in internal medicine. At the time of my interview at Kansas Medical Center, I was told that I would be the only Black intern there. I almost wanted to change my mind about doing my internship there, but I remembered what I had gone through in medical school as the only Black student in the class and should be able to tolerate mostly anything that could come my way. I accepted the internship.

In June of 1974, I received my MD degree (another blessing), and I was so happy that my mother lived to see me obtain all of my degrees—my Bachelor of Science and my Master of Science, both in Tuskegee, Alabama, and my medical degree from the University of Wisconsin in Madison, Wisconsin. I finally fulfilled my promise to her that I made at the age of eleven, that one day I would become a doctor.

My mother was so proud of me but never appreciated the role she had played in all of what had been accomplished. All the whippings, the encouragements, and demands that I do the best that I could at all times were the things that made me determined to succeed. Without my mother's help when she mortgaged the house for ninety dollars, along with my brother's help, I would not have been able to enroll at Tuskegee Institute, and none of this would have been possible. I hope I was able to pay her back in many ways.

One of the most devastating moments in my life was when I received a telephone call on January 10, 1996, at the age of eighty-three, that my mother had collapsed and died.

Chapter 15

Internship and Residency, Kansas Medical School

At the time of my visit to Kansas University Medical Center, I was told that I would be the only Black in the department as well as the other departments. This frightened me at first because I remember being the only Black in my medical school class at the University of Wisconsin. I didn't know whether or not I wanted to go through the racial pressure again. After I voiced my concerns to the chairman of the department at KUMC, he assured me that I had nothing to be concerned about.

The town was impressive, and everyone appeared to be very nice and friendly. In June 1974, I became an intern at KUMC in the department of internal medicine. Later, I started experiencing some of the same things I had experienced in Wisconsin but slightly different in that I had students that I was responsible for training. However, some of the students still wanted to challenge me on everything. I still had to convince them that I knew what I was teaching them. This was not new to me; this is what Blacks in a White society have to endure. Having a Black intern was new for the students, staff, and patients. As months passed, things changed slightly, however, it came out in other ways, throughout the hospital experiences. The resident who was over all the interns of the department of internal medicine showed some racial tendencies. I remember at the end of my internship, one of the interns was on call, but I was forced to take call to allow the other intern to go to the commencement program. I was very upset and voiced this to him and to the department of medicine. Another racial incidence occurred in the department of radiology. As an intern, I had to go over X-ray and discuss them with the students for each patient. I took my students to the x-ray department to review one of the patients' x-rays, and the x-ray tech did not want me to stand in the x-ray room while she looked for the x-ray as other interns were doing. I was told by the tech to "get out."

The head of the department was also called, and he ordered me out of his department. This almost developed into an altercation between us but was stopped by another professor, who advised me to go and report the incident to the chairman of the department of internal medicine. The chairman of the department of internal medicine demanded an apology from the chairman of the department of radiology. These are a few of the racial encounters that I experienced doing my internship. Since my experience, other Black interns have gone through the department and had little or no problems. All the interns and residents had to rotate through the Veterans Administration Hospital. This experience was a much more relaxing with less racial tension. I completed my internship and residency at Kansas University Medical Center in June 1977.

Following completion of my Internship and Residency and obtaining my Missouri and Kansas license, I decided to do emergency medicine in two hospitals in Independence, Missouri. I had done some moonlighting during my residence at KUMC. The money was good for someone just getting started. I had no overhead.

After a few weeks, I decided that I did not want to get up at 5:00 a.m. to be at work by 6:00 a.m. I wanted to start office practice. Starting office practice required money for rental space and office supplies. This was very difficult for me right out of medical school. I tried to obtain loans from a bank and was turned down; I did not know what I was going to do.

Chapter 16

Beginning Private Practice

One Sunday morning, my wife and I decided to go sightseeing in Kansas City, Kansas. I was in Kansas on Minnesota Avenue when I received a call. The caller stated that a pharmacist had given her my name. She was looking for someone to take over her husband's practice, who had just died in an automobile accident, which had occurred only three to four days prior to the call. I asked her where the office was located, and she said on Eighteenth and Minnesota Avenue, and she asked me to meet her at the office.

As we were looking at the office, she handed me the keys and asked me not to open the office until after her husband's funeral. I asked her how I was going to pay her; she said that we will work that out later.

There were thirty to forty patients scheduled on the books. I saw about that many on my first day at work with the help of his nurse practitioner, of whom I hired. She was a tremendous help to me; she knew the patients very well. This was another blessing.

I did solo practice from 1977 till 1985. I thought if I hired an accountant, all my finances in the business would be handled. Boy was I wrong! My accountant sent me a letter stating that he was retiring. So I hired another accountant to handle my affairs. I found out that I owed the Internal Revenue thirty thousand dollars in back taxes, and we had two weeks to pay it. I tried to borrow the money; several banks turned me down, except the one where I had my business account. They loaned me the money to pay the taxes. This was a very frightening time for me; just the thought of me losing my home that we had built in 1978, which was only four years old, was scary. Debt haunted me for many years, and I had to refinance my house on several occasions to pay bills. Although office practice was very good, there were always things that required money for the office such as rent, supplies, staff, payroll taxes, one son in college and another graduating from high school. Trying to do solo practice was very difficult to do. I was on call twenty- four hours a day, seven days a week; I knew something had to change.

There was another Black internist who was also solo practicing. He and I had been sharing calls and had become good friends. In 1985, we decided to become partners and bought a building at 1604 Minnesota Avenue, Kansas City, Kansas, and renovated it. It was there we started our first partnership and practiced internal medicine until 1991, at which time we sold our practice to Health Midwest, a large medical company in Kansas City, Kansas, and Kansas City, Missouri.

Managed Health Care had a significant impact on health care during the eighties and nineties. These large insurance agents contracted with large health organizations, forcing small groups to join these larger groups. In 1991, we joined Health Midwest and became a member of Midwest Multispecialty Group in Kansas City, Kansas, and Kansas City, Missouri. Health Midwest owns several hospitals and medical clinics in the Kansas City, Metropolitan Area. They were interested in developing a large minority multispecialty group in the Kansas City, Metropolitan Area, consisting of internal medicine, pediatrics, obstetrics and gynecology, and family practice. MMPG consisted of fifteen to seventeen doctors; we were paid based on productivity. This group was started in 1991.

Ten years later, Health Midwest was bought out by another large corporation called HCA. This company bought most of the hospitals in the area and had a total of 235 hospitals in the country. The number of doctors who were members of MMPG on the Kansas side had decreased down to three internal medicine doctors, which shifted the overhead coverage to three doctors. This had a tremendous effect on our income. A failure to get HCA to shift the financial overhead from the doctors led us to pull away and start our own group, which was called the Internal Medicine Group. We again paid ourselves based on productivity, and we soon became concerned about the overhead and distribution of profits.

Doing the summer of 2006, I experienced several health issues, and had cervical spine surgery, After a follower-up appointment, my wife and I stopped by one of her favorite shopping places and I passed out in the store, I was rushed to the hospital, and told that my heart stopped beating, it was beating, too slow, and I needed to have a dependent pacemaker. This frightened me, and made me realize that I needed to move my office practice closer to home to avoid long drives to and from work. I joined MMPG in Kansas City MO, which was much closer to home.

In 2009, I was told that HCA was converting over to electronic records. This meant all medical transactions were to be done by computer, but I never learned how to use a computer. Doctors were to be paid still on productivity, and I had always been called a slow doctor. I believe in giving the patient adequate time, but with the new computer system, patients would only be allowed about fifteen minutes. It would have taken me that long to figure out what to do on the computer. In 2009, I was forced to retire from office practice and started a doctor home visit practice. I found this to be very rewarding and much more relaxing and away from the pressure of the big corporation insisting on me seeing a certain number of patients per day. Productivity was driving how much time you spent with the patient and had a tremendous effect on the doctor- patient relationship, which I always took pride in. Doing home visits made me realize why I was drawn toward the medical profession. I did not anticipate the possible changes that medicine would take.

Manage Care came on the scene in the eighties. Insurance companies started contracts with medical groups to take care of their patients. This allowed the insurance companies to have significant control of the care of larger groups of patients, and larger doctor groups were able to contract with insurance companies. This forced solo practice and small groups to join larger groups. This dynamic caused some instability of health care especially for individual doctors and small groups. It was this kind of culture that created a financial instability for me and many other doctors.

Chapter 17

The Reality of Medical Practice

My initial goal of becoming a physician was to be able to help others, specifically minorities who had been left behind and found themselves in a state of desperation. As a poor country boy from a large family, I looked forward to being able to live a better life and be able to afford things for my family that I was not able to enjoy during my childhood.

I still find myself fighting to get ahead having spent sixteen years in some form of educational training. I experienced heavy indebtedness through both undergraduate and graduate school and continued through medical school with large federal loans. I do not remember ever being debt free. I find myself in a rich man's profession but still with debts, poor, and never felt free to enjoy the luxury that many of my colleagues enjoyed. This is considered professional poverty.

I must recognize the fact that I was able to raise and send my three children to college and very pleased that they did not have to endure what I had to endure as a child; however, I wonder sometimes whether this was a good thing for them and wonder if they appreciated the sacrifices my wife and I made to make sure they had a better life than we did. They never had to work to go to college, and they had the clothes they needed to wear, also the cars to drive, and anything else, including the luxury of a good school.

However, there was something I did not allow them to do. I never believed that one should buy things because of a brand name but instead what was considered a good product. I taught them not to buy clothes just because they were name branded but instead that you were neatly dressed, and you look good. This grew out of my own life experiences.

My wife and I invested a lot of time and effort to make sure our children were good, respectable children and that they respected others. I made it a priority to be at all my children's school activities as much as possible. It was sometimes difficult to schedule patients around my son's basketball, football games, and track activities, but I made a special effort to get there for my children. I did not let myself be an absent dad as I had experienced. A great deal of my parenting came from my own life experiences. I love my children, but I did not spare the rod. My mother and father whipped us, and I still feel that their whipping helped shape our lives. I do not know how my mother could have raised seven boys and four girls without what she did. She made us realize early in life that she was in control. It made it much easier later to discipline us.

I have to admit that I developed some of the same skills. As a father, I was not going to allow my children to disrespect their mother or any other adult. The last time I had to physically discipline my sons was when one of them was about fifteen years old. It was his night to wash the dishes; the next morning, they were not washed.

That morning, I was on my way to work, when his mother said to him, "You did not wash the dishes last night, what happened?"

He responded, "I had other things to do. I did not have time to wash the dishes."

I was entering the kitchen at the time. I dropped my briefcase and grabbed him by the collar and before I could think I was going to hit him with all the force I could, my daughter prevented me from hitting him. He was so frightened. I never had any more problems with him. I believe that husbands should not allow their sons or daughters to disrespect their mother.

However, looking back over the situations; I am not suggesting that physically disciplining of children is the modern- day way of disciplining children. I find myself asking why I, at times, resorted to physical disciplining of my children, but then I remember that this was all I knew having been raised under that type of environment I was raised in. Today, I would advocate a different approach to disciplining children, and I hope that each generation will do a better job of raising their children and learn from our mistakes. I try to set a good example for my children because I never had a father around for most of my life. My adult life has always been haunted by my early life experiences. One can dress up the outer body and make it appear to be something that it isn't. But the inner soul and spirit of a person is the total sum of many life experiences.

Chapter 18

My Spiritual Journey

As indicated earlier in this book, we were a church going family. My sisters, brothers, and I were forced to go to Sunday school every Sunday. We would sometimes try to come up with excuses like my stomach hurts, headaches, but we had to go even if we had to lie on the pews. I grew strong in my belief and dedication to the church and later became a Sunday school teacher. This experience prepared me for a lifelong relationship with God.

During my struggles in college, had it not been for Christ in my life, I would not have been able to succeed. My wife would always find a church for us to worship every Sunday. At that time, denomination was not a priority, however, later, we joined and remained as African Methodist Episcopal (AME) Church members. I would not have made it without Christ in my life. His guidance, protection, and strength sustained me through life's struggles. All of those painful experiences during my early life prepared me for life's obstacles. I do not know what happened to me along the way, but many people saw things in me that I could not see in myself. I have tried to treat everyone as I would want to be treated and tried to be an example for my children and others. Many times, people I knew would call me Rev. Fullard. Once I was at Home Depot, standing at the checkout, this gentleman asked me if I was a minister. I told him no, and his response was that I missed my calling and that I was supposed to be a preacher. These are the type of statements I would get frequently from people that I did not know.

Later, through BHCC, I developed friendship with several ministers. When I was asked to give medical talks in churches and community centers, many would say I gave a sermon. I have tried not to sound like a preacher when I give talks, but it always turns out the same even though the topic would be about health issues. All of these experiences made me wonder, Did I really miss my calling? Was God speaking to me in a way that I was not aware? I thought that when ministers talked about how they were called by God to preach, that God really talked directly to them, and I guess that was what I was waiting on. I later realized that God had been talking in many ways through all the experiences that I mentioned earlier. Was I so out of touch or self-centered that I had missed God's message to me to preach the gospel and share all the miracles that I have experienced during my life struggles?

I have talked about how Mother disciplined us by whipping us when we did wrong. These whipping actually shaped our lives and kept us out of streets and jail. I believe God whipped me in another way when I am disobedient. Sometimes, we do not see the connection and continue our same ways.

As I stated earlier in this book, it was the spring of 2006, I had gone to see the doctor for follow up on my neck surgery, and my wife drove me to my appointment. On the way home, she suggested that we stop by one of her little "junk" stores, and I passed out. That was a very frightening experience for me. After I recovered, I wondered if this was God's way of whipping me for not being obedient to his calling. I prayed for forgiveness and promised to serve in other ways, by being an example for others and serving in the church when possible.

I realized that there are other ways of worshipping— by singing in the choir, organizing the men in the church, and getting them more involved in the worship service, and to help young men see the roles that they can play in church. I could never give back as much as I have been given through the years. My whole life is composed of nothing but miracles from God. That is the only way I can understand and express my life story.

"What does God have to do with it?" Everything. For I would not have made it without God in my life. He takes care of all things that seem impossible. You have heard about my family and economic conditions and to be able to go to college was definitely a miracle.

There was no financial way that I could have gone to college and obtain a graduate degree without the miracle of God. He gave me the strength and endurance to sustain and overcome all of the hardships that I experienced. I was not supposed to go to college and graduate, but I did. This was a miracle. Somehow, I was able to return to Tuskegee Institute one year after receiving my Bachelor of Science degree in biology. I had worked one year as a high school teacher in Denton, Maryland, and then I was able to enroll in a master's degree program at Tuskegee Institute, Alabama. My chance of doing this was very low. We had gone from a two- income family to a one- income family. I had a wife and a son with no financial way of supporting graduate school. But God saw fit for me to obtain financial support through a grant at Tuskegee that enabled me to go to school and support my family with my wife's help. For a poor boy who had no chance of going to college, this was another miracle.

I believe that God does everything his way. He knew that I had promised my mother that I would be a doctor one day. God was preparing me step by step to reach my goal. If you are the son of a rich family, you can make decisions about what you want to be in life and plan to do it without financial concerns. But when you are a son of a poor family, you may have goals, but it's only through the grace of God that you can see your way of obtaining your goal.

After receiving my master's degree, God led me to Stillman College and allowed me to teach for two years. At Stillman, I was placed in a position to receive a Ford Grant that allowed me to apply and attend the University of Wisconsin to work on a PhD in anatomy and physiology, another miracle in my life. How could I have imagined a poor boy from Wrens, Georgia, now working on a PhD degree? There is no end to what God can do. He was aware of my goal all the time, and he, again, put me in a position to move forward to reach my goal. After enrolling in the PhD program at Wisconsin, it was an incident of the bombing of the pharmacy building at Wisconsin that led me to approach the Ford Foundation to receive approval to utilize my grant money for medical school, instead of a PhD degree. This was approved, and I finally was able to pursue my ultimate goal, to become a doctor and fulfill my promise to my mother. Yes, another miracle from God. I believe in miracles.

"All things are possible with God." I do not believe that I alone had the knowledge, endurance, will power, and financial capability to accomplish what I was able to do. I was able to overcome the financial obstacles and education deficiencies that was obviously a factor along this journey.

Chapter 19

Family Dynamics

Our family consisted of seven boys and four girls who managed to survive severe poverty conditions and racial challenges. I would contribute our success to our strong mother who had to endure physical and mental abuse for many years. My father was a man who responded to his surroundings and inability to adequately provide for his family by getting drunk every weekend and would take out his frustrations on our mother. We knew that every weekend he would come home and start a fight with my mother, usually over not having the food he wanted to eat. We all knew that Mother would be physically beaten, and there was nothing we could do, except pray that she would survive the beating. We would prepare for this every weekend. When the beatings were severe, Mother would have us pack our clothes in boxes or bags, and we would walk five miles to our grandmother's and would stay there several days until my father talked Mother in to returning home. This occurrence was predicted to occur almost every weekend. However, one night, my oldest sister, who usually served as our mother when our mother was not around, became tired of watching my mother being beaten by my father, and during a fight between my mother and father, my mother was being beaten badly, my sister picked up a board with a nail in it and hit my father in the forehead. And the beating stopped.

My mother and father were separated for several years before they divorced, and my father moved to Florida. I must have been in my early teens at that time; and the next time I saw my father was at the time of his death. My mother later re-married and had one additional child. Making the number of children eleven, seven boys and four girls.

It is still a wonder how my mother was able to raise eleven children considering the economic conditions at that time. She stressed good character, respect, and neatness at all times. However, our family did have other problems; two of my sisters had children out of wedlock. My second- to- the oldest sister had four children out of wedlock, three boys and one girl. These children were raised by my mother as her own children; this sister followed in our father's footsteps and became an alcoholic, which was later responsible for her early death. One other sister had a boy out of wedlock at a very early age. I believe that it was my mother's strong religious beliefs that gave her the strength and courage to raise eleven children plus five grandchildren.

We were members of the AME Church, but because of being close to a Baptist Church, we would walk there to Sunday school every Sunday. Mother insisted on participation in all church activities.

My grandmother was a Seventh- Day Adventist member who would walk around the community, passing out material and trying to convert others to the Seventh- Day Adventist faith. It was after I went away to college when my mother was converted to the Seventh- Day Adventist faith. Later, several of my sisters and brothers were converted to the Seventh- Day Adventist faith. I remember coming home from college and having to experience the doctrine of the Seventh-Day Adventist Church. My mother would not cook pork, which we were raised on. We would have to sneak away and buy a barbecue sandwich and eat it before returning home. My mother was dedicated to the Seventh- Day Adventist faith. She, along with others, raised money to build the first Seventh- Day Adventist Church in the Black community in Wrens, Georgia.

I cannot explain how my mother was able to raise sixteen children, but I believe her strong faith in God was most important. My family has always been a close family who supported each other. Without the support of my brother who was in the air force, I would not have been able to register for college that led to my success. Our individual successes were a family success, and all of our family members have done well and have come a long way.

Four of my brothers went into the armed forces and used it as a catalyst to advance their lives and career. This allowed them to pursue farther education. I have often made the statement that all of my brothers and sisters were much smarter than me but taking advantage of opportunities may have played a significant role in the direction we chose to take, recognizing that there was nothing to do in Wrens.

After graduating from high school, it was so important to get away as soon as possible. Many of our friends, classmates, and others in the community were not that fortunate. I am so thankful and proud of my family's accomplishments.

One of my brothers had formed a pact with four of his classmates to join the service one week after graduating from high school. All of them were accepted, and one week after graduating, they left Wrens for the air force. I do not know what would have happened to us if we had remained in Wrens for any period of time after graduation. Most of us received further education, and that allowed us to pull ourselves out of a poverty- stricken environment that could have affected our lives in such a negative way. We did not let poverty define us. The thing that we hated about our mother was the beating, her insistence of neatness, studying, picking cotton all day while other students were in school, but these were the things that later shaped our lives and brought us out of poverty.

My Family

Pictured: Back row, Left to right

Americus, James, Steve, Samuel, Jasper, Robert, William.

From row: Left to Right:

Ada, Mother Carrie, Barbara, Mattie, Not pictured, Louise.

Chapter 20

*The Children
(My Sisters and Brothers)*

1. Mattie Ruth Fullard McFarland (a.k.a. Mattie Ruth) was the eldest child of the Fullard family. Mattie played a very important role in taking care of the family when mother was at work. Sometimes, she was stricter than our mother. She would break up fights between us and whip us if needed. Mattie was also there to help break up fights between Mother and Daddy. After graduation from high school, she moved to Philadelphia, Pennsylvania, to live with relatives. She later married and had two girls. She was not able to go to college but was very supportive of her sisters and brothers as they pursued their education. After the death of her husband, her health deteriorated, and she died of a neuromuscular disorder at the age of seventy-five.

2. Americus (a.k.a. Merk) Fullard) was the oldest boy of the family and was the first one who had to endure Daddy's alcohol abuse problem, which was the reason that Merk dropped out of school and moved to Philadelphia, Pennsylvania, to live with relatives and later joined the army. After returning to Philadelphia from the army, he married and had three children, two boys and a girl. He learned several skills in the army, including auto mechanics and electricity, business skills, and plumbing. He had several small businesses and worked for the City of Philadelphia for several years. Merk was killed in a "manhole" while working for the city; he was forty-four years old. The family greatly missed Merk who was the leader of the family and the one we all depended on financially and for advice. Although he did not go to college, he was a very smart businessman.

3. Louise Fullard (a.k.a. Sister). Sister, as we all called her, was the third born; a very stubborn and mean person with very low self-esteem, who probably had some mental deficiency, which made it impossible for her to maintain a job. There was no psychological or medical help available in the little town of Wrens nor was my family able to afford it. Because of low self- esteem, alcoholics took advantage of her, and she became an alcoholic and also had four children out of wedlock. Mother tried to control her behavior but was unsuccessful. Mother took care of her children as if they were her own. Alcohol controlled her life, and she later died from an alcohol- related disorder at the age of forty-six. Her children all grew up to be good, respectable citizens and were able to develop a good life for their families.

4. Robert Fullard (a.k.a. Bob), the fourth born, graduated from high school and joined the air force one week after graduation. He has been so supportive of the other family members and would give you anything he had if you needed it. He was a good example of what Mother taught us, very neat and well- dressed all the time. Bob obtained several skills and training in the air force, including business management and administration. He has helped several of us in college, and I have given him credit for helping me be able to go to college. I would not have been able to enroll at Tuskegee without Bob's help. He is one of the most unselfish persons I know, and I owe him a lot.

After the air force, Bob married several times. But only had two boys and one girl by his first marriage. Bob lives in Decatur, Georgia, with his lovely wife.

5. Ada Fullard Kirby is the fifth born and the third girl of the family. Ada graduated from high school and moved to Philadelphia to live with relatives, later attended Oakwood Seventh-Day Adventist College in Huntsville, Alabama; she graduated with a degree in business administration and a master's degree in business. She later married and had three girls; she worked at the college until her retirement at the age of eighty-three. Ada was always devoted to the Seventh- Day Adventist Church.

6. Jasper Fullard Jr., MD. My story has been illustrated in this book. I am the sixth born to the Fullard family. I was named after my father. I am married and have two boys and one girl. Please read this book for more of my story.

7. James E. Fullard was the seventh child who was considered our father's "pet." He was responsible for many of the whipping that we received. Daddy depended on him for all the gossip and family news. James married several times; he had two sons, one each by two of his wives. James graduated from college and received a Bachelor of Science and master's degree in business administration. He became a Seventh-Day Adventist and moved back to Wrens, Georgia, after retirement and later died at the age of seventy-four.

8. Samuel Fullard (a.k.a. Sam) probably was one of the smartest of the family. He was the eighth born into the Fullard family. He went to the army after graduation from high school and received three associate degrees, including auto mechanics, welding, computer science, and other skills. He has been married several times and has seven children. Sam's hobbies are restoring old cars and trucks. He lives in Jefferson County, Georgia. He is also dedicated to the Seventh- Day Adventist Church.

9. Barbara Fullard Jordan (a.k.a. Bobbie), the ninth born and the youngest girl of the family. She became pregnant at the age of fifteen and had to drop out of high school but later was able to graduate after going to Philadelphia to live with her sister, and Mother raised her son. After obtaining her diploma, she later married and had three other children (two boys and a girl). Barbara is a very talented seamstress. She can make anything, and she makes her own patterns. Barbara is a very dedicated Seventh- Day Adventist

10. William M. Fullard (a.k.a. Bill) is the tenth born to the Fullard family and the last born to my mother's first marriage. After high school, he attended college and received a BS and MS degree in psychology. Willie owned his own business as a farmers' insurance managers for many years in Chicago. He was married twice and has one girl and one boy. Willie is now retired and living in South Carolina near his daughter, who has MS.

11. Steven C. Berry (a.k.a. Steve) was the only child born from mother's second marriage. This marriage did not last long; Steve's dad was killed when he was five or six years old. We often tell him he saw his dad about as much as we saw our dad, but we all had our mother. Steve graduated from high school and college. He received a BS degree in business management and was married twice and has two sons and one daughter. He is retired and also has a hobby of restoring old cars, and he also received the State of Georgia Citizen Award.

Our mother was a strong lady who raised eleven children of her own and six or seven grandchildren mostly by herself. They were all treated as if they were just another one of her children. What you were able to eat depended on how fast you made it to the table. I don't know how she did it, but we managed to get something to eat each meal.

Chapter 21

Our Children

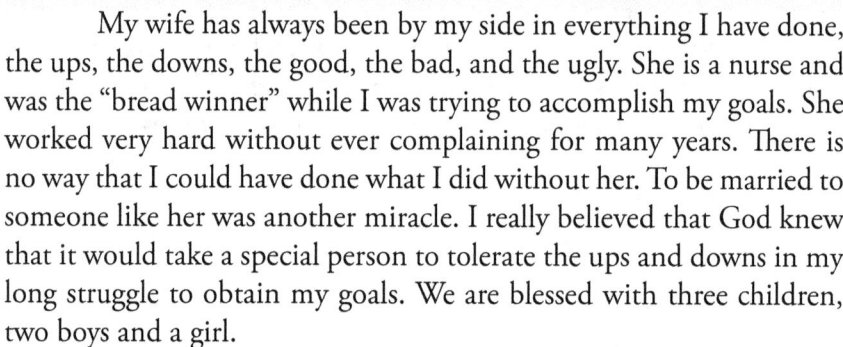

My wife has always been by my side in everything I have done, the ups, the downs, the good, the bad, and the ugly. She is a nurse and was the "bread winner" while I was trying to accomplish my goals. She worked very hard without ever complaining for many years. There is no way that I could have done what I did without her. To be married to someone like her was another miracle. I really believed that God knew that it would take a special person to tolerate the ups and downs in my long struggle to obtain my goals. We are blessed with three children, two boys and a girl.

In June 1963, our first son was born, just before I received my Bachelor of Science degree from Tuskegee Institute. We were not financially ready to take care of a baby, but with my wife working at the hospital, we were able to make it. Watching them grow was an experience. I will always cherish the little things they did growing up. I remember my oldest son wanted a dog, which we initially was not in agreement with, however, when he was five years old, he was given a puppy by a friend in the neighborhood. This was a pretty little puppy that we all grew to love. My son was very rough with the puppy and would carry him around by his neck, not realizing that the puppy was not old enough to be handled this way. He thought he was just playing with him. Later, the puppy became lethargic and died. It was a very sad day for all of us. We had to bury the puppy in the back yard. We decided that we would not get another dog.

When they were growing up, they were very active in sports— soccer, hockey, basketball, football, and baseball. They just had natural ability and excelled in all sporting activities. My oldest son was the quarterback of his high school football team, and he was also a very good point guard on his high school basketball team. He received a basketball scholarship to Arizona Western College in Yuma, Arizona. After two years there, he received a scholarship to the University of Iowa, Iowa City, Iowa. My wife and I made most of the home games to Iowa. He is married to a lovely Japanese lady whose father did not believe in race mixing and was not in favor of her marriage to my son who is Black. The rest of her family respected her decision. They have been married for twenty-four years and have two children, a girl and a boy. Both children are very smart and very athletic. My grandson is a very good baseball and basketball player and has generated a lot of local and national news that led to several scouts monitoring his progress. This publicity led to his grandfather on his mother's side to become more interested in meeting him. So finally, at the age of fifteen, his grandfather and grandmother came to visit them in Iowa City from Japan to watched him play baseball. My wife and I also went to Iowa City to meet them for the first time. Their expectations changed after we were able to meet and talk about their daughter and the grandchildren. We explained to them how much we loved their daughter and would always treat her as if she was our own, and they did not need to worry about her and our grandchildren. Our granddaughter is very athletic too, and she is very good in violin, gymnastics, soccer, and basketball. Before we left Iowa City, we were invited to visit them in Japan. I believe we were able to show them that we are a good family that respected every one's culture and differences and our love for our daughter-in-law and our Japanese connection.

In March 1966, my second son was born just before I received my master's degree in zoology from Tuskegee Institute. He was the dare devil of the family. When he was a teenager, he had a bicycle accident. He just had to have the latest twelve-speed bicycle that had just come out, and I bought it for him. He had not ridden it more than three or four times when he and a neighbor friend decided to challenge each other to a game of chicken. Each would leave from opposite ends of the street, and each would try to see who would move over from the center of the street first. The one who moved first was the chicken. I was at home when I heard the ambulance siren in the neighborhood. Soon, there was a knock on the door. I was told that my son was involved in an accident and was hurt. I picked up my little black bag and ran up the street; there was my son lying on the street with blood on him. My son was taken to the ER and found to have a fractured clavicle on the right side; his friend received several stitches. The twelve-speed bicycle was gone forever.

He also played all kinds of sports—soccer, hockey, basketball, baseball, and football. And he seemed to be a natural in all the sports he played. He loved to jump, and he would prefer to jump over twelve to fourteen steps than to walk down them. At home, he would jump from the second floor to the first level, instead of walking down the steps. He loved to jump and later became a very good pole vaulter in high school and earned the title of becoming the number one high school pole vaulter in the nation and held the record of eighteen feet and a half inch until his graduation. He received a scholarship to Arizona State University for pole vaulting, however, he never reached in the area eighteen feet and a half inch again. He later transferred to Kansas University in Lawrence, Kansas, and continued his pole vaulting till graduation. He works here in the city and has never been married. Throughout our children's years in school, we tried to make it to their activities as much as possible. Sometimes, my wife had to go alone because of my schedule at work.

In May 1970, while working on my PhD in anatomy and physiology in Madison, Wisconsin, our daughter was born. During her teenage years, we were faced with another challenge— our daughter decided she wanted a dog. We held out until she was babysitting for a doctor in our neighborhood, who had a dog that had puppies. He brought one to the house for her, and she convinced us to let her keep the puppy. She did not keep her promise of taking care of the dog. The dog started chewing up furniture, rugs, and shoes, and my wife grew very impatient with the dog and suggested that he be tied outside on the porch while we were at work. That worked for a while One day, we returned home, and the dog was not on the porch. Someone had cut his leash and he was gone. I had the challenge of trying to look like I was interested in finding him.

My daughter and I went through the neighborhood looking for the dog but were not successful. Later, she convinced me to purchase a hamster for her, which was also a challenge just to keep him in the cage. Once he was lost for months, then one day, he appeared in the kitchen looking very healthy. He would get lost almost weekly. Later, we found him in a trash can in some water. We had to conduct another funeral service in the back yard, tears included. This was the last pet that we allowed in the house. My daughter was very good in music (piano). She received many awards in competitions. She is also a very good soloist, and she did not care much for sports but did support her brothers. After high school, she attended the University of Oklahoma, majoring in microbiology. It was harder for me when she went off to college than the boys. She did not like living in the dormitory, but she had to stay on campus for her freshman year. When it was possible, we allowed her to move out and live with two friends off campus. But we were constantly getting calls about the other roommates, eating up her food and wearing or stealing her clothes, and the apartment caught on fire. She wanted to live alone off campus and had found a town house with security that she liked. My wife and I went to visit and agreed to rent this town house for her but not fully thinking about the other expenses, such as furniture that would be needed. She wanted matching furniture with a black dinette set with glass top and black chairs. We looked for hours for the furniture that she wanted, and finally, we were able to find a glass- top table. After hours of looking, I picked the glass top up to put it into the truck and dropped it on the pavement and broke it. We had to make arrangements to have another glass top made for the table. We were very pleased with the town house and furniture that we were able to find; but my daughter stated that she needed to practice piano, and she was taking music courses, and she needed a piano in her town house. She did not have access to the one in the dormitory anymore.

She was also a member of the Traveling College Concert Choir and, sometimes, directed and accompanied the choir; we were able to find her a black piano.

After she moved off campus, she complained that she had to walk from the library at night after the buses stopped running, and she was afraid. Guess what? Daddy bought her a car. My daughter still tells everyone that my daddy spoiled me. I do not regret what I did for my children. I never forgot my struggles in life and could not think of my children ever going through what I did. However, looking back over my children's lives, I am certain that I overreacted and did things for them that one may consider to be "overboard." Our hard work and support for our children paid off. We have three children that have made us very proud; they are always very respectable, kind, and friendly children, who are always willing to do anything to help others. I believe this is what we had hoped for in our children. Another blessing from God.

My daughter married a White/Italian young man, whom I was not initially in agreement with. My daughter had very few young men to come to the house. I found out later that she was afraid that I would not approve of them. One day, we were in the kitchen when I heard someone outside blowing the horn. I asked my daughter who that was, and she answered that it was a friend of hers that she liked. I asked why he was blowing his horn and not coming to the door. She stated that he was afraid that I wouldn't like him. I told her to call him in, and I wanted to talk to both of them. I was born in the South and had experienced lots of racism, and this was still haunting me; so, it was hard for me to approve of my daughter dating or marrying a White man. I explained this to him and that I did not approve of the interracial marriage because of potential problems with others mistreating my daughter. I remember telling him that if they really wanted to get married, that I would not object, but if I ever hear of him mistreating or calling her out of her name, I will kill him. In retrospect, I realized that this was a bad thing to say, but I had flash backs of my own experience in the South.

Years later, we gave our daughter a very beautiful wedding. His family was there, and I got a chance to meet them for the first time. After meeting his family, I began to regret the things I had said to him. We have become good friends with his family. I then realized that my daughter would be okay. They have three very beautiful and smart children. My son-in-law was the right person for my daughter; he is an excellent provider for my daughter and my grandchildren. I realized that I was wrong for prejudging him and thinking that he was just like some of the other White men. He is the best son-in-law anyone could hope for. I am so proud of my daughter and her husband for the way they are raising their children. They are all "A" students in school and participates in church activities. As I consider how I felt about my son's wife's father, and the way he did not want to accept her marriage to my son, I realized that I was a hypocrite for how I felt about a White man marrying my daughter. If we would allow our daughters to marry who they want, everything would be all right.

We have six grandchildren, three girls and three boys. I don't think I mentioned that my son-in law had a son before they were married. He is growing up with our other grandchildren and is just like our own. He went to national guard training after graduating from high school and attended Kansas State University. All are in good health, and when we get together, it looks like an international family. God has blessed us again with a good family, brought together by God.

Kenneth's family

My oldest son

Left to right: Kenneth, Izaya, Keiko and Reiko

Karri, Family

Pictured Left to right

Laylana, Erik, Karri, Jasper, Devontre, Gianna,

My Family:

Kenneth Patricia Karri Jasper Cedric.

Chapter 22

Facing Racism

Having lived in the little town of Zebina, Georgia, we were constantly exposed to racism. Blacks soon learned their place in the community, and the Black males all had the same name, "Colored boy." We watched our father constantly being degraded by being called those names. We experienced him working so hard for very little pay, and the only response he could give was "Yes, sir boss!" This was a hard thing to hear having a large family to provide for and not being able to earn enough to provide food, shelter, and clothes for his family. We watched him become an alcoholic for this was his way of dealing with an impossible situation. Racism destroyed his life and had the same effect on the whole family. We were born into racism, and our lives were negatively impacted by the pressure of racism.

Racism is very visible when one considers the education situation in Zebina and Wrens, Georgia. The schools were dilapidated buildings with small, crowded rooms with little or no heat or air-conditioning. The student- teacher ratio was higher than in Black/White schools. There were no lunches; the few books that we had were old and outdated, which were received from the White schools that were too outdated for them to use. Occasionally, we would receive old half- spoiled cheese and fruit from the White schools. There was little or no school supplies that could be used by the students.

In spite of all of the deficiencies that the teachers and students experienced at Wrens High School, a great deal of emphasis was placed on how we scored on the national test when compared to our White counterparts. We were considered inferior and incapable of learning and competing with the White students. One may think about the racial differences in schools and the lack of supplies that we had to endure. Racism affected every aspect of our lives, and this did not support good self-esteem and positive life outcome. Racism played a significant role in our economic status in Zebina and Wrens. The only jobs available were farm work (chopping and picking cotton) for two to three dollars a day (three dollars per one hundred pounds). We worked hard picking one to three hundred pounds per day. Sometimes, the price was decreased if the boss felt that the cotton was dirty, and we had to accept his decision. The Fullard family worked so hard and would usually pick a bail of cotton a day, and we became very popular with the farmers in the area.

This experience was probably the closest experience to slavery that one could experience in the nineteenth century, hard work with little pay. But in spite of this condition, we worked hard to provide for our family. This was a very depressing and challenging time in my life with very little hope and aspirations. I could not visualize anything positive beyond the cotton field. My concern was that my name would always be "boy or colored boy" My self- esteem was low, and there were no professional mentors that we came in contact with. My aspiration to become a doctor was through an experience I had with a White doctor who mistreated my mother and almost caused her death. This aspiration was not because I saw him as someone who I wanted to be like, but someone who I did not want to be like. But instead, I wanted to help the people that he did not want to help. This negative experience inspired me to do something good in my life. I discovered that out of powerlessness and low economic situations, one can find motivation and inspiration to improve their overall situation and reach their goal in life and propel them out of a trapped poverty and racial era. My struggle was born out of a racial society that has destroyed so many goals and aspirations for so many Blacks. There may always be struggles, but what you do to overcome these struggles is so important to one's accomplishment in life.

The struggle has produced both pain and gratification throughout my life. I had many dreams of financial gratification, a dream of the big house, the cars, the clothes, and vacations, also being aware of all things that I had deprived my wife of, including clothes, jewelry, and social experiences. I often reflect on the times that we had little or no food to eat. There are times when I wished for a whole piece of chicken to eat without having to share with my sisters and brothers. I could not forget being able to afford my own clothes that were not "hand- me- downs." Having to spend many years in school, I did not think that there would be any gratifications for my struggles. Because of many years in school and the financial deficit that was created, the hopes and reality of financial gratification was minimized.

The loans created and debts continued to have a tremendous financial effect for many years after I started to practice medicine. This had a great effect on the expectation on how lucrative the practice of medicine was supposed to be. For many years, I was still paying off bills that had accumulated over the years. Sometimes, I had to refinance the house to obtain money to pay off bills and pay loans. I had never gotten a chance to experience the full financial success of a physician when compared to many of my colleagues. So the myth that all doctors are rich is certainly not true as it relates to me. The struggles to reach my goal were both painful and gratifying. However, there are so many other great benefits in being a physician that has been so rewarding to me. Success is not just financial, but the ability to help so many people with their medical problems. I never refused to see a patient based on their ability to pay. I also focused on the community and volunteered to do many health projects in the community. On several occasions, I would give the patients credit for their co-pay in order for them to be seen. The co-pay was a stipulation by the insurance company before the doctor could see the patient. Most of the doctors refused to see Medicare and Medicaid patients because of very little financial benefits.

Chapter 23

Community Outreach

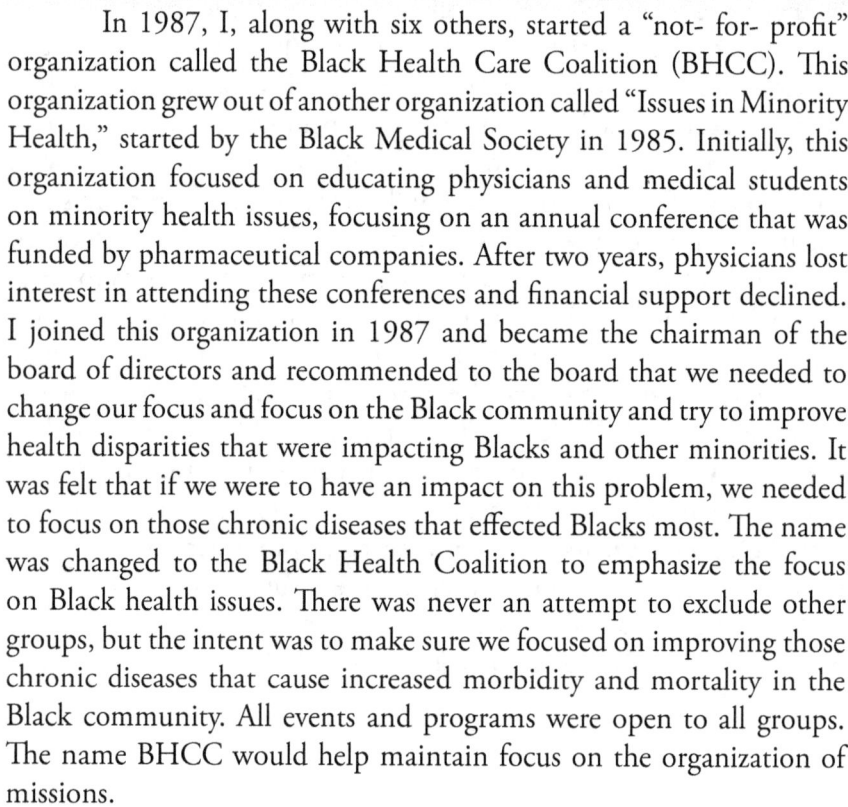

In 1987, I, along with six others, started a "not- for- profit" organization called the Black Health Care Coalition (BHCC). This organization grew out of another organization called "Issues in Minority Health," started by the Black Medical Society in 1985. Initially, this organization focused on educating physicians and medical students on minority health issues, focusing on an annual conference that was funded by pharmaceutical companies. After two years, physicians lost interest in attending these conferences and financial support declined. I joined this organization in 1987 and became the chairman of the board of directors and recommended to the board that we needed to change our focus and focus on the Black community and try to improve health disparities that were impacting Blacks and other minorities. It was felt that if we were to have an impact on this problem, we needed to focus on those chronic diseases that effected Blacks most. The name was changed to the Black Health Coalition to emphasize the focus on Black health issues. There was never an attempt to exclude other groups, but the intent was to make sure we focused on improving those chronic diseases that cause increased morbidity and mortality in the Black community. All events and programs were open to all groups. The name BHCC would help maintain focus on the organization of missions.

In 1987, the BHCC started with six board members consisting of nurses, physicians, and one dentist. I was the chairman of the board for the lack of anyone willing to serve as the CEO and president. I had to serve in these areas as well. Meetings were held in the office of Stay Well Visiting Nurses Inc., a nursing service owned by one of the board members. Later, we moved the meetings to a nursing home facility of which a board member, who was the vice president of BHCC, was the manager. In 1987, we became incorporated in the State of Missouri.

We organized screening programs that were conducted in churches and community centers. These programs focused on hypertension, diabetes, and hyperlipidemia. We also started doing workshops and seminars on chronic diseases that impact Blacks more than non-Blacks. This was the main reason that the organization was named the Black Health Care Coalition, to make sure the focus was on those chronic diseases that impacted Blacks more than non-Blacks. Initially, we did have a discussion about the possible effects that the name could have in obtaining funding for the organization, but we felt that it was important to focus on the group that is impacted the most by these chronic diseases. We never wanted to exclude anyone who needed to take advantage of the program that we conducted.

We were able to obtain smaller grants from the state, city, and county. By using volunteers to conduct health programs, we were able to do several screening programs and educational workshops on chronic diseases. HIV and AIDS became a big issue, especially among Blacks who thought that it was a White man's homosexual disease. The BHCC felt that we had an obligation to do something to educate Blacks about the disease. We were the first and only organization in the metropolitan area to focus on educating the Black community about HIV and AIDS. The BHCC, with very little money from the Health Department and the state, organized a program called "Train the Trainers" in HIV and AIDS. We recognized that we would not be able to reach the whole community and that we needed to train people who would have contacts with a larger group of people. We were able, with volunteers, to train teachers, social workers, nurses, doctors, policeman, beautician, barbers, ministers and one bishop on HIV and AIDS.

The Black Health Care Coalition became well- known in the community for our efforts to improve health care in the Black community. Later, my employer, Health Midwest, agreed to give the BHCC space in one of their facilities. This space was developed into a very large office space with additional space for educational activities.

Health Midwest was later bought out by another large company, HCA, the owner of approximately 235 hospitals in the country. We were able to expand our relationship with many other organizations in the area. It was very important that we focused on the Black church, the center of the Black community. I arranged and met with the Black ministerial alliance monthly to educate them on HIV and AIDS and other chronic diseases that impact Blacks. Ministers from different denominations were present. We were later able to conduct workshops and many educational programs in the churches on HIV and AIDS and chronic diseases. As a result of these programs, many churches started their own HIV and AIDS programs. Many ministers preached about HIV and AIDS as well as other chronic diseases.

The BHCC developed a strong and respectable relationship with the Black churches in Kansas City, Metropolitan Area, which allowed us to do many different workshops and screenings in the churches. This relationship led to applying for a federal grant to continue the church screening programs. At this time, the BHCC had been proven to be capable of conducting large healthcare projects as a not- for- profit organization.

In 1995, we applied for a federal grant of $600,000 to develop preventive healthcare centers in five Black churches in the metropolitan area. The grant was awarded with a mandate that we, at least, have 1,500 encounters in the five centers for the three years duration of the project. After the end of three years, we had over ten thousand encounters, and this was considered a very successful project. We provided each center with a registered nurse and one assistant with equipment to do blood sugars, blood pressures, and cholesterol, as well as educational material to conduct educational workshop and to do discussions on hypertension diabetes, cardiovascular risk factors, and HIV and AIDS. After the federal project was completed, the centers continued by the churches with the BHCC overseeing and assisting when needed. After the grant project, we started several other projects, including the church health watch program, focusing on specific health projects for each church. These included focus on breast cancer, prostate cancer, HIV and AIDS, diabetes, hypertension, and other chronic diseases. Usually, these were conducted at the request of the churches. We also organized small committees in the churches with the pastors' recommendations to focus on health issues in their churches. This later led to forming a steering committee by the BHCC consisting of representatives from each participating church. The committee met at the BHCC office monthly. The purpose was to allow the churches to participate in the health issues that their churches were interested in for their congregation.

In the late nineties, we developed breast cancer and prostate cancer programs; we identified in thirty to forty churches in the area that would allow us to conduct five- minute talks on one Sunday of each month on blood pressure, breast cancer, prostate cancer, diabetes, HIV and AIDS. The BHCC was able to find doctors and nurses that agreed to participate in this project. They were given short messages on these subjects to emphasize during regular church services. For breast cancer, each woman in the church would be given a carnation flower with instructions on how to obtain a free breast exam and a free mammogram if needed.

It has always been difficult to get Black males to obtain prostate exam, and we had to come up with creative ways of getting them to a doctor for an annual examination. Recognizing that they would get a haircut regularly, we started a special project involving the barbers. Several barbers were invited to a special meeting and were educated about the problem of getting Black men to annual exams and the role they could play in helping us educate them about prostate cancer. They were all willing to participate, and a brochure was made with a picture of barbers and doctors and information about the project. The brochure contained instructions on how Black males could obtain a free annual exam. There was also a hotline telephone number that they could call and be scheduled for a free exam. Special hats and aprons were created for the barbers and pins were given to the men receiving the exams. There were approximately three hundred to four hundred Black males who received free annual examinations and were encouraged to continue their annual exams each year. In order to do this project, we had to get approximately forty-five doctors in the area to agree to give one to two free exams each week. One of the largest national labs agreed to do the blood work free for this project or at a reduced rate. The BHCC objective was always to identify what was needed in the Black community and find creative ways of dealing with the problems.

In about 2003, we had to create ways of funding a secretary and executive director, which took a lot of work and responsibility from me. I continued to serve as chairman of the board until 2013, after the new board members felt that they could take more responsibility. One of them agreed to take on board leadership. I also felt that they were able to lead the organization in the direction that we needed to go. I continued on the board as the past chairman of the board. I strongly believed that with a very strong and capable executive director and president, it was time for new leadership with new ideals and abilities so that we could continue to grow as a not- for- profit organization in the metropolitan area. After thirty-five years, the BHCC is still a respected and well- known organization that continues to make a difference in the Black community.

There are multiple health issues that impact minorities more than non-minorities; the BHCC felt compiled to focus on multiple chronic diseases that impact minorities more than non-minorities. Blacks are still dying five to ten years earlier than non-minorities and rank number one when considering morbidity and mortality from diabetes, hypertension, cardiovascular disorders, HIV/AIDS, prostate cancer and other cancers, and all other causes of death and morbidity with exception of suicidal deaths. I recognize the fact that if we are to make a change and decrease the health disparities that exist between minorities and no minorities, we must focus on educating minorities about these chronic diseases. We decided through "the Black Health Care Coalition" to approach these problems by developing preventive health care centers in Black churches. The Black church is the center of the Black community and is the best way to reach a massive number of Blacks.

As chairman of the BHCC, I spent many years, along with the other volunteers, focusing on improving health care in the Black community. During these many years, we faced many obstacles. Funding was a big problem for us. Many times, we had to use our own resources to keep the organization going. We were fortunate to receive some grant money for various programs from the city, state, and later, federal. There was little or no money to pay staff. Everyone volunteered their time and sometimes money and their resources. The BHCC survived in spite of the racial bias we faced from funding agencies, including the city and state. They would usually bypass the BHCC and fund other institutions or agencies, forcing us to contract with these agencies. Most of the money for the project would be used by these agencies for administration, leaving very little money for programs in the Black community. The BHCC is still standing with a very good reputation and has had a big impact on thousands of minorities and non-minorities in the greater Metropolitan Area of Kansas City, Missouri. The BHCC is recognized as an alternative preventive healthcare organization in the Kansas City area, state, and county. I am very pleased with our accomplishments through the years. I believe my mother would be proud of my volunteer service in the community.

I will never feel like I have contributed enough of my time and resources. So many years of my life, I have received so much from others that I could never pay back. My whole life story is based on others helping me in so many ways. The motivation to become a doctor grew out of lack of care for my mother because she was Black. This experience has had such an impact on my life and has helped shape my life today. The way I practice medicine was shaped by my past experiences. I always felt like I could not deny a patient's health care. Practicing medicine has not been as lucrative for me as some other doctors; partly because I wanted to make sure I spent enough time with patients to address their health concerns. Most people feel that all doctors are rich; well, I certainly don't fit in that category. I get great satisfaction in helping people with health problems through my practice or through volunteering my service with BHCC through the years.

We have to give thanks to a number of individual businesses and institutions for the success of the BHCC. The list include, Health Midwest and HCA for providing office space for many years. There are several funders who have made it possible for us to conduct various programs. The BHCC will continue to conduct programs in the community to challenge the city and state to recognize healthcare disparities. I do not believe that Whites will ever accept the responsibility of the effects that slavery had on Blacks, and the increase health disparities they experience today.

This could lead to a more equitable distribution of resources and a better understanding of health disparities. Local and national organization such as the American Diabetic Association, National Kidney Foundation, and heart and vascular national associations should focus more on health disparities when allocating resources for health care.

It is well known that environmental conditions over multiple years can affect genes, expression, and/ or mutational changes. When the question is asked why Blacks have more health problems and why they use more state and federal resources, Whites must consider the possible genetic effect of slavery and take some responsibility for what we are experiencing today. Financial resources must be geared toward bridging the gap of disparity. Local and national organizations, such as the American Diabetic Association and many others, who are focusing on health issues, should have a special focus on minorities and make sure they are included in whatever they do with special consideration of culture differences.

I have served on several boards, including ADA, State Advisory Boards, and many others. Most cases, I would be the only Black on the board. I have always felt that I had a responsibility to be an advocate for minorities. I can remember on the board of ADA, I noticed that their focus was more on type 1 diabetes and not enough focus on type 2 diabetes. The ads usually did not show Blacks and the increasing problems of such complications, such as loss of limbs, blindness, kidney failure, and other vascular problems, that impact minorities more than no minorities. The ads did not show someone specifically Black who had lost their legs or were blind. I challenged the board and later noticed a change in the television ads. Because 95 percent of Blacks with diabetes have type 2 diabetes, and approximately 95 percent of Whites have diabetes are type 1 and usually include a large number of young White children. The ADA wanted to protect the young children from the devastating effects on them by not showing these severe complications of type 1 diabetes that I can understand, but there were a large number of Blacks who were dying from these complications. Having a minority on the board to advocate for minorities was very essential in focusing on the disparities that continue to impact minorities. The Black Health Care Coalition continues to advocate for Blacks at the local, state, and the federal levels.

Chapter 24

Delayed Gratification

The journey was long and hard, full of roadblocks and obstacles that almost derailed what I had set out to accomplish. My hopes and inspirations were challenged many times along the way.

This journey started at the age of twelve, when I watched my mother almost bleed to death from a nosebleed because of racial discrimination by a White doctor who did not want to treat Black patients. I made a promise to my mother that I would become a doctor one day so that Black patients would not have to suffer because of lack of adequate care. At an early age, I became aware of healthcare disparities in the Black community, but at that age, I was not aware of the struggles that I would have to endure along the way. I believed that God had a plan for me already laid out, for there was no other possible way I could accomplish my goals; a poor Black boy from a little country town, a family of eleven children with only two pairs of pants, a sport coat, and shoes with holes in the soles, and not enough money for registration for college. This was not a good way to start a long journey to become a doctor. I believe God had to have planned this journey for me. Although the struggle was hard and most of the time was unpredictable, everything always worked out in time.

On my initial enrollment at Tuskegee Institute, I arrived on campus with less than one-third of the money that was needed for the enrollment with inadequate clothes to wear, which almost led to being sent home for not attending Vesper services. Because of the dean's change of heart, he gave me money to buy shoes and clothes, so I could continue to attend Vesper service. This was the beginning of my career which must have been part of the plan; what a blessing.

Working as a janitor at the campus hospital led me to my wife, who was the right one for my long journey. I do not think this was an accident; this was part of the plan. She suffered and denied herself so much so that I could pursue my dreams. She was denied clothes, jewelry, and the social life that a wife deserves. It took a special woman to endure the obstacles that we experienced along the way. She was willing to delay gratification until the end. Our children also experienced the struggle, but we tried not to let this affect their needs and desires.

After receiving my BS degree in biology, I taught high school for one year, but after one year, I left that job because of the working conditions. I was without a job and was forced to look for a way to take care of my family; everything fell in place. I was able to obtain a stipend from a summer project at Morgan State University. This was "God's plan" that also led to me going back to Tuskegee to get my MS degree. I made connection with a friend who was a teacher at Stillman College, who told me that he was leaving Stillman College for another job, and the position would be available. I applied and was hired to teach biology and general science. After two years, I was offered a Ford Foundation Grant to work on a PhD in anatomy at the University of Wisconsin in Madison, Wisconsin. I could not explain why things were working out the way they were. I believe in God's plan.

At the University of Wisconsin, things happened that I cannot explain. Apparently, someone other than me knew that I wanted to be a medical doctor. I was able to enroll into the school of medicine. I had no means of finance for medical school. The Ford Foundation had never given money for someone to attend medical school. With my persistence and pleasing approach, they agreed to allow me to use the grant that I was receiving for a PhD degree to be used for my medical degree for four years. This was part of God's plan all along, for what other way was there for me to finance medical school and take care of my family? His blessing did not stop after medical school.

After completion of my internship and residency, I had no money to start a practice in Kansas City, Missouri. The banks refused to lend me money for supplies, equipment, and money to rent a space; I did not know what I was going to do. One Sunday, my wife and I decided to drive to Kansas City, Kansas, to look around the area. We were on Minnesota Avenue in Kansas City, Kansas, when my beeper went off, and I called the number. A lady answered and said that the pharmacist had given her my number because I was looking for a place to start my medical practice. She stated that her husband was a doctor in the area and was killed in an automobile accident, and she was looking for someone to take over his practice. Before I could answer, she asked me where I was, and I stated that we were on Ninth and Minnesota Avenue. She replied that the office was on Eighteenth and Minnesota, only a few blocks away. My wife and I met her at the office. We were so happy. This was God's plan at work. She showed us around in the office; everything was there in place all the equipment, supplies, and a full schedule of patients. Her request was that I wait until after the funeral before opening the office. I asked her about the cost, and she stated, "Not to worry about that. We will work that out later." She gave me the keys, and after the funeral, I started seeing patients. I cannot think of any way to explain my life's journey other than "the miracles of God."

This has been delayed gratification for my wife and children and I, but an impossible dream was made possible by the miracles of God. As promised to my mother, I was able to have one of the largest medical practices in the Metropolitan Area, Kansas City. I led a group of medical professionals to organize a not- for- profit organization to decrease healthcare disparities in the Black community and dedicated many hours in the Black community. "The impossible dream was not possible without the miracles of God."

The end.

Blurb

Racism and healthcare disparities have always been a problem in the Black community, especially small country towns. This book illustrates how a poor Black boy at the age of twelve watched his mother almost die from the lack of adequate health care from a White doctor.

I come from a very poor family of eleven children, poor education environment, low self-esteem, and with no Black professionals except for Black teachers to inspire me and other Blacks in the community; but at the age of twelve, I promised my mother that one day I would become a doctor so that Blacks would not have to suffer from the lack of adequate health care. The promise to my mother was "an impossible dream."

By reading this book, you will learn how the miracles of God navigated my crooked journey and how the impossible was made possible, and I was able to obtain a Bachelor of Science, Master of Science, two years on a PhD program before completing a medical degree Along with other health care providers, I was able to organize a not-for-profit organization to decrease healthcare disparities in the Black community.